TREASURES OF THE
BUDDHA

THE GLORIES OF SACRED ASIA

TREASURES OF THE
BUDDHA

THE GLORIES OF SACRED ASIA

TOM LOWENSTEIN

DUNCAN BAIRD PUBLISHERS

LONDON

Treasures of the Buddha
Tom Lowenstein

First published in the United Kingdom and Ireland in 2006 by
Duncan Baird Publishers Ltd
Sixth Floor
Castle House
75–76 Wells Street
London W1T 3QH

Conceived, created and designed by Duncan Baird Publishers

Editor: Peter Bently
Designer: Rebecca Johns
Managing Editor: Christopher Westhorp
Managing Designer: Manisha Patel
Consultant: John Peacocke
Picture Researcher: Julia Ruxton
Commissioned artwork: Peter Visscher and Sallie Alane Reason (map)

Library of Congress Cataloging-in-Publication Data is available

ISBN-10: 1-84483-417-4
ISBN-13: 9-781844-834174

10 9 8 7 6 5 4 3 2 1

Typeset in Perpetua and Optima
Color reproduction by Scanhouse, Malaysia
Printed and bound in Singapore

Notes
The abbreviations CE (Common Era) and BCE (Before the Common Era) are
used throughout this book instead of AD and BC respectively. Dates given
for archaeological and cultural periods are only approximate.
All measurements given in maps and diagrams are approximate.

Captions for pages 1–3
Page 1: The *dharma* wheel, a prominent motif in Buddhist decorative art,
architecture and sculpture.
Page 2: A standing Buddha statue of gilded teak within the Ananda
temple (also called Ananda Pahto or Phaya) at Pagan (Bagan), Burma.
The gesture is that of *abhaya mudra* – reassurance or fearlessness.
Page 3: A type of pendant from Tibet that is commonly referred to as a
"mooneater". This magnificent ornament, consisting of gold, turquoise,
lapis lazuli and rubies, was worn by officials and came with a matching
counter-weight. The name "mooneater" was inspired by the subject depicted on it because very little is known about its actual use.

CONTENTS

INTRODUCTION

THE ART OF SEEING

Given the extraordinary diversity of the cultures in which Buddhism took root, the art that this one great religion inspired in those cultures over many centuries is correspondingly varied. But also, uniquely among world religions, Buddhism started as a religion with a leader but without a god. Gautama Siddhartha, the historical Buddha or "The Awakened One," born in the late sixth- or fifth-century BCE (see page 14) in southern Nepal, was a charismatic teacher who, like many other thinkers in India at the time, took little or no interest in the world of deities and spirits which formed part of the accepted cultural and religious environment. What he taught was a series of spiritual truths about the nature of existence, realized during a hard-won and personal experience of enlightenment. It was this enlightenment that took the Buddha from the treadmill of repeated births (*samsara*) to the realization of *nirvana*: a sublime condition in both life and death that was without suffering or taint.

The humanistic and somewhat abstract nature of early Buddhism, combined with the fact that the Buddha and his followers were homeless, wayfaring mendicants, made early Buddhism difficult to represent artistically. In the centuries that followed the Buddha's death, however, the survival of his teaching was ensured by the establishment of institutions which began to enshrine the Buddha's teaching (the Dharma) in monasteries, temples, and the reliquary mounds (stupas) that marked the burials of Buddhist elders. These, around the third century BCE, became the sites of the first Buddhist devotional art. With delightful playfulness, much of this art—such as decorates the Great Stupa at Sañchi (see pages 46–49)—is generously adorned with imagery from Indian nature cults which coexisted with the quietly austere thought of conservative Buddhist monasticism.

THE FIGURE OF THE BUDDHA

At this early stage Indian Buddhist art remained in some respects indirect, and the Buddha himself was suggested only through symbols, such as his footprints (see pages

KEY

⌖ Site associated with the life of the Buddha

▲ Mountain

● Other site

→ Principal Silk Roads

| 0 | 300miles | 800miles |
| 0 | 500km | 1100km |

22–25). By the first century CE, representational Buddha figures evolved. First in Mathura (northern India), and soon after in Gandhara (Peshawar Valley, modern Pakistan). The beautiful and serene Buddhas from the Mathura workshops of the Gupta era have become icons of the perfected being that the Buddha himself represented. This was a human being whose condition approached the divine but whose face radiated the promise to the onlooker of the same possibility of spiritual evolution.

As Buddhism grew in popularity in the first and second centuries CE, the figure of the Buddha became increasingly the object of devotion. To emphasize this came the addition to Buddha figures of hand gestures (*mudras*), which expressed some essential aspect of the Buddha's being or intention, such as mudras of "teaching," "fear-allaying," and "boon-granting." Spreading from India to all subsequent Buddhist cultures, Buddha figures were created with *mudras* that could be read by the onlooker as expressions of the Buddha's wisdom and compassion.

Certain *mudras* came to be adjuncts of certain genres of representation. One widely used genre shows the Buddha in meditation during his enlightenment experience. Sculptures in this genre would often show the Buddha touching the earth (*bhumisparsha mudra*), calling the earth to witness the authenticity of his achievement.

SACRED BEINGS

Nature spirits and *nagas* (serpent deities) were just a few of the nonhuman beings which Buddhist sculptors delighted to represent. By the fourth century CE, sculptures from Gandhara show the Buddha flanked by another genre of supernatural being. These were semidivine *bodhisattvas* (Buddhas-to-be), figures who would play an increasingly prominent role in Buddhist representation, and indeed become central to the arts of China (where the savior figure of Avalokiteshvara evolved a feminized form) and Tibet (where many impressive *bodhisattva* images were elided with images from Indian mythology and indigenous Tibetan folk religion).

THE MAHAYANA

One theme, in this connection, concerns the separation of two great currents in Buddhism. Around the first century CE, new ideas emerged in southern and northwestern India which would spread to virtually all the lands reached by the Dharma. Those who embraced this different vision of the goal of Buddhist practice referred to their school as the "Mahayana," a Sanskrit term meaning "the Great Vehicle." This alluded to the Buddhist metaphor of the "ferry" that could carry all beings across the river of suffering (*samsara*) to salvation on the "far shore" (*nirvana*). Mahayanists described earlier schools of Buddhism as "Hinayana" ("Lesser Vehicle") because, they claimed, according to those schools only a minority of spiritual adepts (*arhats*) who had achieved enlightenment were destined to reach that far shore.

The Mahayana had both a popular and an abstruse, speculative character. In popular Mahayana, the ideal of the *arhat* was replaced by that of the *bodhisattva*, an "enlightenment being." As opposed to the human and generally monastic *arhat*, the *bodhisattva* was a being of the imagination, a sublime, semidivine manifestation of Buddhist compassion who vowed to refuse entry into *nirvana* until all other beings had been saved first. And while *arhats* are certainly depicted in the art of many traditions, it was the figure of the *bodhisattva* which most vividly captured the Buddhist imagination. Thus with the Mahayana, Buddhism became a religion of salvation which held the

ABOVE

The Ruwanweliseya *dagoba* (2nd-century BCE) at Sri Lanka's ancient capital of Anuradhapura. The Sri Lankan *dagoba* is one of many forms into which the Indian stupa, or reliquary monument, evolved.

OPPOSITE

Aizen, a god of Shingon, Japan's Tantric Buddhist sect. Although not theistic in the Judeo-Christian sense, Buddhism embraces many divine beings that often began as personifications of qualities such as compassion and wisdom. Lacquered and painted wood, ca. 1400.

promise of comfort to the suffering populations of India's growing urban centers. This promise of salvation was expressed most vividly by the arts and, whether in stone sculpture, painting, or temple architecture, the protective function of the Mahayana outlook was most powerfully conveyed by the presence of compassionate and wise *bodhisattva* figures. Some form of Mahayana Buddhism came to be practiced in Tibet, China, Japan, Vietnam, and Mongolia.

THE THERAVADA

Only one of the early non-Mahayana schools survived to the modern era: the Theravada, which remains the dominant form of Buddhism in Sri Lanka and southeast Asia. (It is uncertain whether Mahayanists included this school in their somewhat disparaging term "Lesser Vehicle," and Theravadins generally dislike the term.) The art of these ancient Buddhist cultures is based less on *bodhisattva* images—although elements of Mahayana iconography were reflected in Theravada cultures—but on the person of

the Buddha and those aspects of his biography on which monastic discipline is modeled. Meditating and teaching Buddhas dominate the sculpture of Sri Lanka and southeast Asia. Gold, applied to sculpture and to temple architecture, was sometimes used to express the nobility of the Dharma and to demonstrate the generosity of donors, many of whom came from the ruling classes.

This book is designed to guide the reader through all the significant phases of Buddhist thought and art, and traces the evolution of Buddhism through the cultures of Asia, offering an overview of ways in which the Dharma was interpreted and how Buddhist ideas were translated into beautiful and diverse artistic forms. Chapter One thus introduces the reader to a survey of the Buddha's own life, the fundamentals of his teaching, and ways in which early Buddhism was related to Indian thought of the time. Chapter Two outlines the way Buddhism became established in India and how it spread to the northwest and from there, dramatically, along the Silk Road into Central Asia.

The flow of Buddhist ideas to Sri Lanka and southeast Asia is the subject of Chapter Three. Chapter Four dwells on the arrival of Buddhism in China and its spread first into Korea and from there to Japan. Finally, in Chapter Five, the reader is introduced to the extraordinary transformation of Indian Buddhism into the cultures of Tibet, other Himalayan regions, and Mongolia.

Throughout this survey, sculpture, architecture and painting are discussed in their relationship to the ideas and beliefs of Buddhist religion and philosophy as they evolved throughout Asia over the centuries that followed the foundation of the Dharma.

chapter 1

ORIGINS

BUDDHA, DHARMA, SANGHA

OPPOSITE
Early Indian Buddhist art denoted
the Buddha by symbols such as
his footprints, as on this limestone
panel from the Great Stupa at
Amaravati (1st century BCE). Each
footprint bears various auspicious
symbols, including *svastikas*
and a wheel representing the
Buddha's teachings, or Dharma.
Another symbol on each heel
represents the "Three Jewels" of
Buddha, Dharma, and Sangha.

BUDDHA: THE AWAKENED ONE

THE LIFE OF SIDDHARTHA

Both history and legend inform our knowledge of the Buddha. On the one hand there are the legends surrounding the Buddha's previous incarnations (*Jataka* stories) and his miraculous birth, on the other there are accounts of his life as a human being who vigorously participated in the social and philosophical world of sixth- and fifth-century BCE India. Sometimes, of course, legend and history intertwine, and our understanding of Buddhist history is much enriched by this variety of sources.

The Buddha ("Awakened One"), also known as Shakyamuni ("Sage of the Shakyas"), was born as Gautama Siddhartha into the family of a Shakya chieftain at Lumbini in the Himalayan foothills of what is now south Nepal. His birth is tradition-ally placed ca. 566BCE, though recent archaeological evidence has inclined many scholars to date his birth somewhat later, to ca. 483BCE. The legend of the Buddha's birth is akin to that of many hero sagas. When his mother, Mahamaya, dreamed that a beautiful white elephant had entered her womb, palace soothsayers predicted the birth of a child who would become a *chakravartin*, or "wheel-turner"—either a universal emperor or a great teacher who would renounce the world.

FROM PRINCE TO RENUNCIANT

Fearful for the succession, Siddhartha's father confined the boy to an existence of secluded luxury, banishing signs of human misery from the royal estates at Kapilivashtu, and marrying him to a cousin who bore him a son. But higher powers intervened. As, on four successive days, Siddhartha rode through the palace grounds, the gods, who knew that the prince was troubled by the meaning of

A sculpted slate relief of the Buddha with four of his early disciples. Above the disciples two divine beings make the gesture of reverence (*namaskara* or *anjali mudra*). The Buddha, seated in the "lotus" position on a lotus-decorated throne, makes the fear-allaying gesture (*abhaya mudra*). Gandhara, 2nd or 3rd century CE.

existence, presented to him "the Four Sights"—scenes of suffering which would prompt the young prince to renounce his privileged life and seek the truth. These were a decrepit old man, a sick man, a corpse, and lastly, a serene ascetic wanderer.

Repelled by the sights of suffering and enthralled by the image of the holy man, Siddhartha abandoned his wife and child and fled the court in the dead of night—legend has it that deities held up his horse's hooves so that they would not clatter on the road. He shaved his head, adopted a yellow mendicant's robe, and sought spiritual peace as a hermit, before studying meditation with a brahmanical master. Still dissatisfied in his search, the future Buddha joined a group of five ascetics whose aim was to eliminate bad *karma* through self-mortification.

THE AWAKENING

Close to death after six years of severe austerities, Siddhartha determined on a gentler path. Having eaten some rice, he withdrew to the base of a pipal tree to meditate. For forty-nine days, repelling the assaults of Mara, the Evil One— the embodiment of desire—he sat in the meditation which culminated with his "awakening," or "enlightenment," thereby transforming himself from a *bodhisattva* ("one destined for enlightenment," "future Buddha") to a Buddha ("one who has woken"). Convinced that he had identified the cause of suffering, the Buddha, now aged thirty-five, gave his "First Sermon," expounding the outcome of his meditation to his five former partners in asceticism in a deer park at Sarnath, near Varanasi. This event is also known as the "First Turning of the Wheel of the Dharma." For the next forty years or so he traveled through the kingdoms of Kosala and Magadha in the Ganges plain preaching his new doctrine, the Dharma ("teaching" or "truth"), to his growing community of followers, the Sangha.

ABOVE
The head of the fasting Buddha from Gandhara. It was in this northwestern region of the subcontinent, perhaps under Hellenistic influence, that the earliest images of the Buddha as a human being are believed to have been made. This piece (2nd or 3rd century CE) is unusual even for the naturalistic Gandharan sculptural tradition.

The biography of the Buddha is described in narratives interfusing folklore with an earthy naturalism that gives a vivid picture of ancient Indian society. Some of the legendary material focuses on miracle-working, which the Buddha occasionally practiced but discouraged in his followers. One tale describes how the Buddha, having converted his father, wife, and son, engendered the malice of Devadatta, a first cousin. However, when Devadatta unleashed a dangerous elephant in the Buddha's path, it kneeled obediently before the master. Another story takes the Buddha to the "Heaven of the [Deities]" where he preached to his mother and descended to earth on a jeweled ladder (see also pages 30 and 37). Buddhist legends have a host of gods appearing at important moments throughout the Buddha's life, attending his birth and supporting his actions, or protecting him from harm, like the great snake deity Muchalinda, who is depicted towering over the meditating Buddha.

But equally compelling are the moments in the Buddha's biography when he is shown as an ordinary man. He rises from sleep, washes, takes his robe and bowl, and walks out on alms rounds. He disputes sharply with Brahmins and rival teachers. He swims effortlessly in the Ganges. He takes his food with lay devotees such as the courtesan Ambapali and the blacksmith Chunda.

As the Buddha entered extreme old age, he vividly compared his own body to an ancient cart held together by frayed straps. When finally, at the age of around eighty, he contracted food poisoning from pork donated by Chunda, one of his followers, the physical agony of his final hours was accompanied by spiritual tranquillity. As he neared death, the Sangha, despite its philosophical commitment to equanimity, mourned openly the loss of their great teacher. Most poignantly, his faithful attendant Ananda leaned against a door-jamb, disoriented and weeping.

A recumbent Buddha in Cave 26 of the Ajanta cave complex in modern Maharashtra, India (see Chapter 2). This cave contains a prolifically decorated *chaitya* (shrine) hall and two monastic dwellings (*viharas*). The 6th-century relief carving is 22 feet (7m) long and shows the Buddha at the point of his death and entry into "final *nirvana*" (*parinirvana*). The modeling of the Buddha's head and torso are in Gupta style, suggesting the serenity of a human being whose perfected inner life is expressed by a harmonious physical beauty. The lower section shows Buddhist devotees in mourning.

DEPICTING THE MASTER

OPPOSITE

The 1st-century CE east *torana* (gateway) of the Great Stupa at Sañchi, originally founded by the Indian emperor Ashoka in the 3rd century BCE. The rich carving on this *torana* includes elephants and an exquisite *yakshi* (nature deity) who leans out from a tree in the lower right-hand bracket.

BELOW

A carved limestone panel from Sañchi showing a Wheel of the Dharma (*Dharmachakra*) and four Buddhist devotees. The wheel also represents the Buddha, who would not be depicted as a human being until ca. the 1st century CE.

The earliest visual representations of the Buddha date from about the second and first centuries BCE. The earliest specifically Buddhist art is found on carved limestone panels on the great stupas at Bharhut and Sañchi (see pages 46–49). In addition to a profusion of decorative motifs drawn from nature and folklore, the majority of these carvings celebrate the lives both of the Buddha and his previous incarnations.

However, the time had yet to arrive for the Buddha to be represented as a human being—the earliest images, such as those at Sañchi, denote the Buddha's person and episodes of his life through nonrepresentational symbols. Most strikingly preserved in carvings on stupas are symbols suggesting the Buddha's presence, his birth, enlightenment, the doctrine as first expounded at Sarnath, and his death. Two main signs suggest the Buddha's presence. The first is an empty throne, alluding to both the Buddha's royalty and his renunciation of power. The second is stylized footprints (*Buddhapada*) such as those preserved at the Sañchi and Amaravati stupas. Wheel symbols symbolize the Buddha's teaching, "The Wheel of the Dharma."

Two trees also figure in this iconographic series. The *shala* tree, on which the Buddha's mother leans, is used to suggest the Buddha's birth, while a *bo* or *bodhi* tree—the name given to the pipal under which the Buddha sat in meditation—is the symbol *par excellence* for the enlightenment (*bodhi*). Small stupa domes, frequently incised on stupas themselves, symbolize the Buddha's death and entry into *nirvana*.

A further image suggests both the Buddha's high caste and spiritual pre-eminence. Before his birth, it was predicted that he might choose to become a "universal emperor" (*chakravartin*). Hence, early icons include mythological *chakravartin* figures flanked by symbols such as the royal wheel and umbrella, while the elephants of stupa iconography also suggest lordly power and the Buddha's conception. These are balanced by lotuses, which allude to the purity and tranquillity of Buddha and Dharma.

Alongside such symbolic images, nonhuman earlier incarnations of the Buddha, as narrated in *Jataka* tales, are lovingly represented. Illustrating one *Jataka*, sixteen carvings of the Buddha as a mythic elephant that sacrificed its six tusks are crowded onto a crossbeam of the south gate of Sañchi.

THE BUDDHA AS HUMAN BEING

The first anthropomorphic representations of the Buddha evolved more or less simultaneously at Mathura in north central India and in Gandhara during the first century BCE. Mathura figures show naturalistic, often quite earthy, standing and seated Buddhas, formally akin to the representation of nature spirits of earlier tradition. Gandharan imagery was influenced by Greek artists who had followed Alexander the Great into the northwest frontier from the early fourth century BCE. These, too, were lifelike, but often stiff and semi-European in feature and dressed in Greco-Roman robes. *Jataka* narratives remained popular subjects, but were now focused on human

representation. A biographical genre also evolved showing, for example, the Bodhisattva emaciated by his pre-enlightenment austerities (see page 16) and dramatic compositions of the dying Buddha attended by his Sangha (see pages 19–21).

A purely Indian art evolved at Mathura in the second and third centuries CE, which created Buddhas that were beautiful in a new way. Inspired no doubt by the growth of Mahayana, these figures, often backed by a halo in complicated lotus patterns, were both hieratic and compassionate, sensitively alive and yet suggestive of an abstract metaphysical ideal.

The climactic development of this genre emerged during the Gupta period (ca. 320–480CE), the "Golden Age" of the Indian arts (see pages 50–55). Aesthetically, the Buddhas of this era attain exquisite and sensuous perfection, but, like the huge *bodhisattvas* painted on the cave walls of Ajanta of the same period, Gupta Buddhas also radiate inner spiritual life. They at once meditate, teach, and bestow reassurance. This, finally, was a Buddha form that exemplified the psychological impact of his doctrine.

DHARMA: THE TEACHINGS

THE PATH TO NIRVANA

OPPOSITE

The Buddha preaches the *Lotus Sutra*, one of the central scriptures of Mahayana Buddhism, on the Vulture Peak at Rajagrha (present-day Rajgir in Bihar, India). The mountain is represented by the rocks surrounding the Buddha, who is flanked by disciples and the *bodhisattvas* Avalokiteshvara and Mahasthamaprapta. An 8th-century silk embroidery on hemp from Cave 17 at Dunhuang in China (see pages 116–119).

RIGHT

A 5th century CE sandstone relief from Sarnath, where the Buddha first taught the Dharma in a deer park, showing events in his life. His birth (bottom left), enlightenment (bottom right), first sermon (top left), and final *nirvana* (top right) enclose four legendary events: the descent from the Heaven of the 33 Deities (see page 19); a monkey offering the Buddha honey at Vaishali; a miracle at Shravasti; and calming a fierce elephant at Rajgir.

During the forty years of his ministry, the Buddha was one many heterodox north Indian teachers who questioned the orthodox brahmanical teaching—in which lay the roots of later Hinduism—with its emphasis on the worship of deities and sacrificial offerings. But virtually every Indian religious and philosophical tradition shared one overwhelming religious view. This was the belief that all beings, including the gods, were implicated in an endless and wretched treadmill of rebirth (*samsara*), forced to endure lifetime after lifetime and the inevitable suffering that went with it. The Buddha's teaching (Dharma) presented a detailed strategy for escaping *samsara* and entering the ultimately happy nonexistence of *nirvana*: a condition of extinction that followed the "blowing out" of the factors leading to rebirth. The Buddha had, himself, experienced both sensuality and self-denial. Having eaten the rice that had established him comfortably under the pipal tree, his meditation led him to a "Middle Way" that lay between these extremes.

THE FOUR NOBLE TRUTHS AND THE NATURE OF EXISTENCE

The Middle Way, proclaimed the Buddha, was reached through an acceptance of the fundamental insight of his enlightenment experience. This was the Four Noble Truths which assert that life is defined by *duhkha*, or "suffering" (to be understood in the broadest sense as "unsatisfactori-

ness," not simply extreme physical or mental distress); that suffering is generated by desire, or craving; that it is possible to extinguish desire; and that there is an Eightfold Path (a synonym for the Middle Way) leading to that extinction. The Eight Factors of the Path—right view, right thought, right speech, right action, right livelihood, right effort, right awareness, and right concentration—form the heart of Buddhist thought, ethics, and meditational practice. The emphasis on "rightness"—the Pali term means "appropriate"—suggests "well directed," an avoidance of extremes which defined the Middle Way.

This initial formulation of the Dharma was enlarged by two analytic descriptions of the nature of existence. Life, proclaimed the Buddha, is marked by three characteristics (*trilakshana*): suffering (*duhkha*), impermanence (*anitya*), and absence of self (*anatman*, "no self"). To achieve an enlightenment equivalent to the Buddha's, it was necessary, through meditation, to experience these aspects of existence at first hand. (The Dharma, said the Buddha, is defined by what he called "come-and-seeness".) Fully to comprehend and accept these tragic existential factors required equanimity. This, again, could be attained through devotion to the Eightfold Path, and in particular, the development of "right awareness" of the Four Noble Truths.

While suffering and transience (which is a component of suffering), may readily be observed and thereby understood, *anatman* remains the most difficult aspect of Buddhism to grasp. On the one hand it confirmed the separation of the Buddhist Dharma (which denied the existence of soul) from orthodox sixth-century BCE Indian thought and its emphasis on self-purification. On the other hand, it asserted the view that human identity could not be defined by any one psychophysical characteristic implied by personal name, character, or caste status—whose categories the Buddha

repudiated as inequitable and unreal. Instead, the Buddha described the personality as a series of processes in a state of change. This, too, could be comprehended through the development of awareness (*smrti*), one of the factors of the Eightfold Path.

THE LAW OF KARMA

The second of the Buddha's descriptions of life is his analysis of "conditioned origination," which defined the operation of *karma*. *Karma* is the process by which actions have consequences both in this lifetime and in lifetimes to come. In particular, if intentional negative actions are not counterbalanced by positive ones by the time we die, rebirth must follow. The nature of rebirth is determined by the balance of positive actions (*punya*) to negative ones (*papa*). Unless we eliminate the effects of *karma*, we must endure endless lifetimes and suffering.

Through step-by-step analysis, the Buddha took this concept significantly further, and revealed the "chain of causality" or series of dependencies whereby suffering accumulates. At the head of the linked sequence of steps comes ignorance, and it is on account of this spiritual and intellectual darkness that desire or craving, attachment to ideas of self, and thus suffering, or unsatisfactoriness, arise. Once spiritual knowledge is achieved, ignorance is replaced by understanding, the chain of causality is reversed, and there is no more rebirth. Thus the evils of old age, sickness, and death that the young Siddhartha witnessed in the grounds of his palace are extinguished.

ABOVE

A 16th-century Tibetan *mandala*, a symbolic representation of the external cosmos, but also of the inner cosmos of the human psyche. At the center of the *mandala* is the esoteric tantric deity Kalachakra in sexual union with his "wisdom partner"; this represents the union of wisdom and compassion in the devotee (see also pages 198–200).

OPPOSITE

The two sides of a gilded bronze statue of the great celestial Buddha Vairochana, decorated on his upper body with scenes of the cosmic Mount Meru and the Trayastrimsha heaven, and on his lower body with scenes of hell. Chinese, Sui dynasty (581–619CE).

MYTHOLOGY AND COSMOLOGY

While the Buddha offered means for dealing rationally with existential pain, mundane human existence in Buddhist India also took place on a larger stage than earth, and within a cosmos whose structure was described in myths shared by Brahmanists and most sectarians. This cosmic geography changed over centuries and across regions. But many of its features during the early Hindu-Buddhist period provided a framework which informed later Buddhist cultures throughout Asia.

The most specifically Indian element in sixth-century cosmology lay in the geography of earth, which was believed to consist of seven continents, one of which—Jambudvipa, "Rose-apple Island"—was India itself. At the center of this island was Mount Meru, the axis of the universe, on whose summit the deities (*devas*) lived, and around which Surya, the sun god, moved daily. Along with Brahmanists, early Buddhists included the Thirty-Three Heavens in their cosmic map. These were populated both by gods and by the virtuous who had achieved a favorable rebirth. According to Buddhist legend, the Buddha used Mount Meru as a stepping stone to visit one of these heavens, Trayastrimsa (the Heaven of the Thirty-Three Deities), to teach the Dharma to his mother, who resided there (see illustration on page 37).

Below the earth were sixteen hells (*niraya*, "the downward path") where evildoers froze, burned, or were otherwise tortured. Alternatively, they might be reborn as a demon (*ashura*), a hungry, wandering spirit (*preta*), or an animal. These "realms of rebirth" are illustrated colorfully in the Tibetan Wheel of Life, which draws on both Hindu and Buddhist iconography. According to Buddhists and Brahmanists alike, the law of *karma* conditioned the future existence of all beings. But to Buddhists, all existence, present and future, was impermanent. Even the gods were mortal, and their lives were too luxurious to eliminate all karmic residues, so a *deva* was unlikely to attain *nirvana*. The ideal rebirth was in the human realm, because only a human being could permanently escape the treadmill of *samsara*.

SANGHA: THE COMMUNITY

THE FELLOWSHIP OF THE DHARMA

The Buddha's first converts were the five ascetics with whom he had formerly practiced, and these men represented the core of his new community (*sangha*). According to legend, a further sixty young ascetics soon joined them, and the Sangha grew rapidly into a body of monks who would both accompany the Buddha and travel separately on missions of conversion. Many of them had abandoned severe austerities for the "Middle Way," the Buddha's more humane regime of meditation and teaching. But these *bhikshus* (literally "beggars") remained celibate, homeless itinerants. Each monk's possessions amounted to a yellow robe and bowl, with which he begged his food in the increasingly dense population centers of contemporary north India.

The extreme weather of the monsoon period restricted the scope of travel, and during the three rainy months the Sangha settled in parks donated by wealthy supporters. The Pali scriptures (see page 63) locate a number of the Buddha's major discourses (*sutras*) in these retreats, where merchants, kings, and crowds of other lay supporters traveled to hear the master. The primitive huts in which the Buddha and his Sangha dwelled later developed into the first Buddhist monasteries (*viharas*).

MONKS AND LAITY

While complete salvation was only regarded as a possibility for celibate, contemplative *bhikshus*, those who donated land, food, and lodging did so partly in order to acquire "merit" (*punya*), which would erode "demerit" (*papa*)

LEFT
A seated Buddha at the top of one entrance to the Mandalagiri *vatadage* (circular relic shrine) in Madirigiriya, Sri Lanka. The relic was housed in a small stupa in the center of the shrine, which is ringed by freestanding pillars. In Sri Lanka, the Sangha had close ties to the ruler (see page 62), a model adopted in other regions such as Burma and Thailand.

and lead to a favorable rebirth. The Sangha and most spiritual adepts were on the whole of high caste, but the Buddha denied the validity of caste divisions, and the common people were assumed to be capable of moral progress which could also lead to rebirth in heaven. Within the Sangha itself, salvation, or the achievement of *nirvana*, was marked by the attainment, though meditation on the Four Truths, of the status of *arahat* or *arhat* ("worthy one"). Leading monks such as Kashyapa, Sariputra, and Ananda are all named as having achieved this enlightened status. Others were described, according to the degree of their understanding, in terms of the limited number of rebirths they would suffer before entering *nirvana*.

THE SANGHA AFTER THE BUDDHA

Surrounded by his monks and visited by noblemen anxious for relics from his funeral pyre, the Buddha died, as he had been born, beneath a *shala* tree. "All natural things are liable to decay. Strive diligently." With these celebrated final words he passed into *nirvana*. This exhortation concisely summed up the Sangha's relationship to an impermanent world in which it must nevertheless exert maximum spiritual effort.

The Buddha instructed his funerary relics to be placed in stupas (see pages 46–49) that would mark the sites, among others, of his birth, enlightenment, first sermon, and death, and this helped lead to his elevation to semidivine cultic status. By contrast, he instructed the Sangha to scatter into separate and leaderless communities. Inevitably, each separate monastic group developed its own distinct character. In an effort to counter the process of differentiation, a number of Buddhist councils were convened, at which the Buddha's disciples recited his discourses (*sutras*) and monastic codes (*vinaya*).

DIVISIONS IN THE SANGHA

Disagreements among communities, which intensified over the next two centuries, led to the first major division in the Sangha. Initially the community split into the Sthavira (Elders, Pali Thera) and the Mahasangika (Great Assembly), and by the end of the millennium these had further divided into some eighteen other schools. Most of the surviving Pali texts derive from the Sthavira, or Theravada, tradition which established itself in Sri Lanka. And by the first century CE, another significant rift occurred with the emergence of Mahayana, a movement in which emerged many lofty and profound new *sutras*. These, Mahayanists claimed, represented more esoteric teachings that the Buddha had held back from public discourse.

In reality, as several modern scholars have pointed out, the Mahayana and its antecedent schools shared many ideas and often inhabited the same *viharas*. Within any one school of Buddhism, members of the Sangha might hold a number of apparently contradictory views. Such has always been the varied and inclusive texture of Indian religion.

chapter 2

INDIA AND CENTRAL ASIA

THE FLOWERING OF THE DHARMA

OPPOSITE

A mural of sitting Buddhas from Cave 10, the oldest of the richly decorated Buddhist rock-hewn shrines and monasteries at Ajanta in southwest India. Dating mainly from the 1st–2nd centuries BCE and 5th–6th centuries CE, Ajanta's paintings and sculpture influenced not only Indian art but also that of the Buddhist traditions of East Asia. (See also pages 50–51.)

THE FIRST BUDDHIST LANDS

BUDDHISM IN INDIA

One paradox in the history of Indian Buddhism is the connection between the homeless Siddhartha, who proclaimed the doctrine of "not self," and ideas of kingship in ancient India. According to legend, the Buddha himself was destined to become a *chakravartin*, either a universal ruler or a spiritual leader. Born with the thirty-two marks of the *mahapurusha* ("great man"), this Shakya prince chose the path that renounces power (see Chapter One). However, as early texts suggest, the Buddha accepted the patronage of merchants and kings and ordained that his relics should be distributed among the rulers of eight Indian kingdoms. The stupas that held these remains replicated the form of Indian royal burial mounds, traditional symbols of earthly power.

Buddhism could not, of course, have survived without both external patronage and its internal hierarchical monastic structure. Elite monks held authority in the early Sangha and there was a marked separation between monks, who were able attain *nirvana*, and laity ("householders"), who mostly could not. Some schools, such as Theravada, described progressive stages on the path of spiritual attainment, thereby creating further degrees of hierarchy.

EAST MEETS WEST: GANDHARA

The spread of Buddhism was, to some extent, dependent on individual rulers and on the temperament of societies that evolved within particular kingdoms and empires. Three areas of empire on the subcontinent between ca. 330BCE and ca. 600CE—Gandhara, the Maurya empire, and the Gupta empire—particularly affected the spread of Buddhism and the development of Buddhist art and ideas. The earliest of these arose in the region known as Gandhara following Alexander the Great's appropriation of northwest India in 327–326BCE. The cultures of Gandhara, in basically what is today's Northwest Frontier Province of Pakistan, flourished in the four centuries before and after the beginning of the Christian era. Lying between India,

modern Afghanistan, and the lands of Central Asia, Gandhara was subject to imperial incursions from both east and west, and in consequence became a meeting place of Indian, Greek, and Persian political and cultural pressures. After the region's brief conquest by Alexander it was partially colonized by Bactrian Greeks and the Persians with whom Alexander had been at war. The mixed Gandharan populations practiced several religions, and Buddhism—introduced ca. 250BCE by missionaries of the Mauryan emperor Emperor Ashoka—coexisted with Hinduism, Zoroastrianism, and, later, Christianity.

Numerous stupa ruins and rock-carved edicts erected by Ashoka attest to the strong presence and high status of Gandharan Buddhism, but until recently little else was known about Buddhism in the region. Brief inscriptions in the Sanskrit-derived Gandhari language and in the Kharoshthi script indicate the existence of monasteries. A Gandhari version of the *Dhammapada* from the Theravada canon, found in Central Asian Khotan, along with the *Questions of King Milinda*, which records a conversation between a monk and a second-century CE Hellenic king named Menander (Milinda), also attest to the importance of Buddhism in the region. Best known to museum visitors are Gandharan stone carvings in a unique Indo-Hellenic style, in which somewhat stiff but naturalistic figures are depicted with European features and in heavily contoured Greek-style robes. Gandharan sculptors also produced

dramatic friezes of scenes from the life of the Buddha, his family, and his associates: these and many fine Buddha figures were probably the first to depict Siddhartha as a human being (see page 20). Some of these figures show the Buddha at crucial stages of his life, many having curly European-looking hair and moustaches (see page 40).

A spectacular addition to our knowledge of Gandharan Buddhism came in 1994, when a collection of twenty-nine first-century CE birchbark manuscripts were discovered and acquired by the British Library in London. As these manuscripts continue to be deciphered, it has become apparent that most of the original Indian Buddhist literary corpus—*sutras* (the Buddha's discourses), *vinaya* (teachings on monastic discipline), and *abhidharma* (advanced philosophical teachings), collectively known as the *Tripitaka* or "Three Baskets"—had been collated and transcribed in a

ABOVE
This Gandharan panel shows a scene from the Buddha's former life as the king of Shibi. The king saves a dove from a hawk, and offers the hawk instead an equal weight of his own flesh. Here, flesh is cut from the king while attendants wait with scales. Both birds turn out to be gods, who restore the king with many boons in recognition of his generosity.

language other than Pali and in a quite different region. Similar manuscripts, such as the Gandhari *Dhammapada*, found their way into Central Asia and to China but, despite the discovery of Kharoshthi inscriptions in Silk Road excavations, no comparably large manuscript finds have been made.

THE MAJESTY OF THE MAURYAS

The second imperial regime under which Buddhism saw significant development was the Mauryan empire. This had its center in the Ganges valley and extended east to the coast of Bengal and south to the Deccan. The domains (established ca. 320BCE) of the first Mauryan emperor, Chandragupta, were vastly extended to the west and in the southeast by his famous grandson Ashoka (reigned 274–236BCE) after a murderous war in 265BCE against Kalinga in the region of modern Orissa. Repenting for the carnage of the Kalinga campaign, Ashoka erected an engraved column that was probably the first of his famous inscribed "rock edicts." "When the beloved of the gods," as Ashoka called himself, "had been king for eight years, he conquered Kalinga, and 150,000 people were carried off to slavery; 100,000 were killed.... Now Ashoka is intensely concerned with justice and the Dharma." The inscription (in the Brahmi script borrowed from Aramaic, a language widely used in the Middle East) further proclaimed Ashoka's intention to refrain from future atrocities.

Thereafter Ashoka pursued policies which he hoped would identify him with the mythological, compassionate and just *chakravartin* or universal dharmic ruler. Ashoka was clearly an ethical, if not philosophical, Buddhist. As his proclamations suggest, he promoted tolerance and social compassion. Having originally supported the non-Buddhist Ajivakas, he declared: "One should honor another man's sect.... Concord is to be commended so that men may hear one another's principles." On another pillar he announced that "high officials for justice" had been created for all peoples' benefit and happiness. A later edict proclaimed that he had had "banyan trees

planted as shade for beasts, and wells dug and resthouses built every nine miles [15km]." "I have done these things," the emperor declared, "that my people might conform to the Dharma."

The Mauryan empire disintegrated soon after Ashoka's death. But as well as carrying out his ideals in clear conformity to the Buddha's teaching, Ashoka left the world an important heritage of Buddhist monuments. These included the Great Stupa at Sañchi (see pages 21, 46–49) and, it is said, thousands of other stupas. Two of his surviving columns remain major works of art. The best preserved Ashoka column, with its single lion capital, dates from 243BCE and still stands at Lauriya Nandangarh in Nepal, while the most significant was erected at Sarnath at the site of the Buddha's first sermon, "the Turning of the Wheel of the Dharma." This is the pillar with the celebrated capital on which four lions, representing the "lion's roar" of the Buddha's enlightenment, surmount the "Wheel of the Dharma," which the Buddha is said to have set in motion at Sarnath. The Ashokan wheel and lion were adopted as emblems of the modern Indian republic.

THE INDIAN STUPA

ENSHRINING THE DHARMA

OPPOSITE

Votive stupas at Nalanda (near Patna in Bihar, India), the great Buddhist center of learning that flourished from the 6th to 11th centuries. Most are in the traditional Indian form, but the larger central stupa is unusual in its two-story square base with octagonal superstructure, and numerous niches holding sculptures of Buddhas and *bodhisattvas*. In the background are the remains of one of Nalanda's great brick temples.

For some centuries after the Buddha's death, the main devotional artifacts created by Buddhists were reliquary shrines, or stupas, built not as works of art, but as pilgrimage markers and memorials to the Buddha and other Buddhist elders. While these earliest stupas have been lost, surviving examples center on a solid dome, at the core of which lay a casket containing a bone fragment, robe, or bowl of a Buddhist saint, or a short religious inscription. The concealed object served as shorthand for the Dharma, while the stupa itself constituted a sign of the Buddha and his *nirvana*: a reminder of both a holy person and of Buddhist religion and philosophy.

The form of the stupa, with its alternating square and round components, had cosmological significance. Above a square or circular base rose the dome (*anda*); these, in symbolic representation of earth and heaven, represented the universe. Contained within was an invisible "world mountain" joining earth and heaven, while atop the dome stood a square platform, the *harmika*, representing the Heaven of the Thirty-Three Deities, which the Buddha is said to have visited (see page 37). A spire rising from the *harmika* represented the world axis, and surmounting the spire were parasols (an emblem of high status in ancient India), symbolizing the divine powers.

While the dome represented an ineffable mystery to the uninitiated, it was usually surrounded by railings carved with familiar religious symbols and scenes from the Buddha's life, which could appeal to the laity—the plain railing at Sañchi (see below) appears to have been exceptional. An ambulatory, reached through four carved gateways marking the cardinal quarters, also surrounded the dome. Here the faithful processed in a clockwise direction meditating on the scenes depicted on the railings. A pilgrimage to the stupa thus continued with a contemplative pilgrimage around it.

THE GREAT STUPA AT SAÑCHI

With its four gates (*toranas*) thronged with spectacular carvings, Sañchi's Great Stupa is both a masterpiece of early Indian art and one of the world's great monuments.

ABOVE

ABOVE
A limestone carving of devotees praying at the Bodhi tree, beneath which the Buddha attained enlightenment. This early example of Buddhist carving predates the representation of the Buddha as a human being; here he is symbolized by the empty throne and his footprints bearing Dharma wheels. From the Great Stupa at Amaravati, Andhra Pradesh, India, 1st century BCE.

Completed during the Andhra dynasty (first century BCE), Sañchi (in Madhya Pradesh) was originally established by the emperor Ashoka, as evidenced by a representation on the west gate of Ashoka himself on a visit to the Bodhi Tree at Bodhgaya, and by his Mauryan lion and peacock emblems on two of the massive gateway crossbars.

The undecorated surface of the stupa stands in stark contrast to the multiplicity of forms on the gates through which the visitor approaches: the dome serving as a reminder of the sublime and indivisible fact of the Buddha's *nirvana*, while the profusion of symbolic figures on the *toranas* suggests both the efflorescence of nature and the folk religions with which Buddhism coexisted. The most eloquent representations of these nature cults are the female deities (*yakshis*) bracketed into the north and east gateways, in particular the richly erotic *yakshi* who leans from a fruiting mango tree

and whose sensuality is echoed, surprisingly, by the Hindu goddess Lakshmi and attendant water-spraying elephants in a panel on the north *torana*. Similar motifs and
images are found at the slightly earlier, but less complete, remains of a great stupa at
Bharhut, and are part of Buddhism's rich Indian heritage.

But Sañchi is, of course, dominated by more purely Buddhistic carvings illustrating *Jataka* stories of the Buddha's previous lives, devotional scenes, and the wheels,
feet, and *bodhi* trees that at this period were used to symbolize the Buddha's presence
(see also pages 20–23). Given that each gate was the gift of a different donor, Sañchi
also presents wonderful aesthetic variety. In contrast to the freely executed *yakshi* figures, some of the packed scenes on the crossbars were created by ivoryworkers, who
brought intense drama and fine detail to their limestone carving.

ABOVE
The Great Stupa at Sañchi,
showing the stupa dome and
the undecorated railing to the
ambulatory, around which
worshippers moved in a sunwise
(clockwise) direction. Two of
the monumental gates (*toranas*),
with their intricate and crowded
decoration, are shown to the left
(see also page 23). Founded by the
emperor Ashoka, the stupa was
completed in the 1st century BCE.

THE GLORIES OF THE GUPTA

THE GOLDEN AGE OF INDIAN BUDDHISM

The greatest examples of Indian Buddhist art were created during the Gupta period (320CE–ca. 600CE). The Gupta dynasty took its name from its founder, King Chandragupta I, and the three centuries that followed his rule have been described as the Golden Age of north Indian culture. Like the European Renaissance, this was a period in which many arts flourished. As with some European rulers, a number of Gupta princes were themselves artists and scholars. During the Gupta period, as exemplified by the works of "India's Shakespeare," Kalidasa, and the completion in final form of the *Mahabharata* and *Ramayana* epics, Sanskrit drama and poetry reached their zenith. The Gupta also saw a flowering of Hindu and Buddhist temple building, though most of this has been lost. Among surviving examples are the elaborately carved *chaitya* hall (shrine) with its superbly detailed facade in Cave 19 at Ajanta (see below), and the nine-story brick tower, now heavily restored, at Bodh Gaya. The Chinese traveler and scholar Xuanzang (see page 111) described a similarly impressive fifth-century brick temple at Nalanda (see page 47), the great Buddhist center of learning in northeast India , but nothing of this remains.

GUPTA ART AND SCULPTURE

Gupta graphic art is most memorably represented by the great wall paintings and softly carved sculptures at Ajanta and Ellora in present-day Maharashtra province. An isolated and dramatic gorge on the bend of a river, Ajanta consists of thirty caves excavated from solid rock into monastic dwellings and *chaitya* halls. The two colossal *bodhisattvas* in Cave 1, suggested the great art historian A.K. Coomaraswamy, attained a perfection "in which the inner and outer life are indivisible." In the presence of these larger than life but weightless figures, we experience a visual manifestation of the *bodhisattva's* compassion and detachment, as evoked in the Mahayana *sutras*, which were being written during this period. It is tempting to imagine that the Gupta artists had in mind the *Heart Sutra*, which describes the *bodhisattva* Avalokiteshvara "coursing in

RIGHT

The great pyramidal tower, 180 feet (55m) in height, that rises above the Mahabodhi ("Great Enlightenment") temple at Bodhgaya near Patna, modern Bihar province. The temple was erected in the late Gupta period next to the spot where the Buddha sat in meditation before gaining enlightenment; the structure that survives today, although much restored since the late 19th century, essentially retains its original form. Marking one of the four great pilgrimage sites associated with the Buddha's life, the Mahabodhi was also one of the most influential of all Buddhist monuments, inspiring sacred buildings elsewhere in the Buddhist world. The finial with its umbrella-like spire is a motif derived from stupa architecture.

RIGHT

This sandstone figure of the high Gupta period (5th century CE) is one the supreme masterpieces of classical Indian carving. The Buddha is seated in the lotus posture making the *dharmachakra-mudra,* the gesture that sets in motion the "Wheel of Dharma" and symbolizes his teaching of the Middle Way.

deep wisdom which has gone beyond," but who still gazes down on earthly life with profound insight and compassion.

Perhaps the most sublime creations of the Gupta are freestanding Buddhist sculptures. Some scholars maintain that these achievements were made possible only after Indian stoneworkers had assimilated naturalistic Greco-Roman representation from Gandhara. Certainly, as with the painted *bodhisattvas* of Ajanta, suggests Coomaraswamy, we have in Gupta figuration the culminating classic phase of the Indian imagination, "at once serene and energetic, spiritual and voluptuous," in which "energy proceeds from within the form." Whether or not the humanistic representational impulse originated in Gandhara, the Buddha of Gupta imagination—as also transposed by Singhalese, Indonesian, and Cambodian stoneworkers—is both human and sublime: a convergence of the earthly and divine that has perhaps never been exceeded by artists in any tradition.

THE RISE OF THE MAHAYANA

The achievements of Gupta art were the expression of two main currents. On the one hand lay the inspiration of painters and sculptors who brought the finest elements of previous traditions to the culminating realization of a "national art." On the other, there were new ideas that expanded the Buddhism of the earlier period. These ideas were contained in the Mahayana (see Introduction), a development that took many forms—some popular, some learned and abstruse—which would have far-reaching influence as it spread to East Asia, Indonesia, and Tibet.

Scholars believe that the Mahayana ("Great Vehicle") developed in south India or in the northwest of the subcontinent, and that it evolved in discussion rather than in dispute with existing Buddhist traditions, which Mahayanists came to refer to as Hinayana ("Lesser Vehicle"). Though all Mahayana texts postdated the historical Buddha, some Mahayanists claimed that these writings represented special teachings that the Buddha had withheld, but which had been magically preserved by *naga* (serpent) deities in an infernal kingdom. Some of these *sutras* are highly poetical, such as the *Pure Land Sutra* (*Sukhavativyuha-sutra*), a Sanskrit work evoking a Western paradise or "pure land" accessible to all the faithful. This was the *sutra* that became most closely tied to the salvationist Pure Land sects of China and Japan (see Chapter Four). Another hugely influential work was the *Lotus Sutra* (*Saddharmapundarika-sutra*) which also taught a compassionate and all-embracing Dharma.

At the Mahayana monasteries in the south and northwest, and at the Buddhist university at Nalanda in modern Bihar state, a tougher and more speculative Dharma emerged from the writings of philosophers such as Nagarjuna, Vasubhandu, and Asanga, who explored many of the powerful and profound doctrines relating to notions of selfhood and "emptiness" propounded, but not fully developed, in earlier Buddhism. Nalanda itself was the greatest center of Buddhist learning for at least six hundred years until its decline in the twelfth century. Earlier Mahayana texts composed in the major Indian monasteries and in Central Asia in the first centuries CE included the enormous literature of the school called *Prajñaparamita* ("Perfection of Wisdom," or "Wisdom that has gone beyond"), of which the brief *Heart Sutra* (see page 155) was a summary.

Although Indian Buddhism succumbed to pressure from Hindu revivalism and Islamic invasion between the sixth and twelfth centuries CE, and great libraries such as that at Nalanda were destroyed, the Mahayana took on new life in China, Korea, Japan, and Tibet. Thus, while this vital new movement enjoyed only a short existence in its homeland, all schools of Far Eastern and Tibetan Buddhism owe their origin to it.

OPPOSITE
The full features and the serene, contemplative expression of this 5.25 inches (13cm) high gilded wooden Buddha head from Central Asia reflect the sculpture of the Indian Gupta period. The tightly curled hair leading to a topknot, the long earlobes, and the round *urna* on the forehead, which once held a gem, also derive from Indian stone carving tradition. From Tumshuk (present-day Xinjiang province, China), on the northern branch of the Silk Road, 5th–6th century CE.

A LOST BUDDHIST WORLD

THE DHARMA IN THE LANDS OF THE SILK ROAD

BELOW
Buddhist monk-scribes depicted in an 8th-century wall painting collected from a Silk Road monastery at Karashahhr by Sir Aurel Stein. The monks are in a cave writing with brushes on prepared palm leaves. Their faces show the integration of Indian and Central Asian styles which was typical of Silk Road painting.

The history of Buddhism in the vast region of Central Asia that separated Gandhara and western China is the story of both movement along the Silk Road and settlement in substantial urban and monastic centers, such as Kashgar, Kucha, Turfan, and Khotan that lay east of Samarkand. But most of the terrain through which traders and monks made their way to Dunhuang in western China (see pages 114–117), and back again, was a wild and imposing landscape of mountains, difficult passes, and, not least, the stony Taklamaklan and Gobi deserts—a difficult journey, at best, of more than three thousand miles (5,000km).

To the challenge of the terrain and desert climate must be added frequently changing tribal populations of nomadic hunters and herdsmen, as well as Turkic, Arab, Tibetan, Uighur, and Chinese rulers with their frequently shifting alliances and unpredictable attitudes toward itinerants and their property. Nevertheless, until the eleventh century, when sea routes to China from India and the Middle East rendered such heroic overland journeys superfluous, many thousands of travelers survived, grew rich, and, not least, took ideas and religion to some of the remotest places on earth.

BUDDHIST MISSIONS

Buddhism was not the only religion to travel the many arid wilderness tracks, to the north and south of the Tarim Basin, that constituted the Silk

Road (see map, page 7); Christians, Jews, Manicheans, and, by the eighth century, Muslims also followed these paths. As happens along trade routes, religious beliefs might be spread inadvertently by passing traders, who might in turn be converted to other religions encountered along the way. In the case of Buddhism, though, the task of conversion fell not to merchants but to Indian, Gandharan, and Sogdian missionaries who transported Buddhist texts and teachings along the same lonely trade routes and established communities in many Central Asian oasis towns, thus creating centers of both scholarship and devotion that generated the first populations of Buddhist converts beyond the Indian subcontinent.

The spread of Buddhism from Gandhara through this region and eventually to China probably started before the first century CE. The earliest Buddhist missionaries were probably of the Dharmaguptaka and Sarvastivadin sects from the mountainous region of Sogdiana, to the north of Gandhara, while priests from the regions of modern Afghanistan and Kashmir probably carried Sanskrit Mahayana literature to Buddhist centers such as Khotan during the same period. The result of this relatively small but constant migration of missionaries and pilgrims was manifold. On the one hand, it spread ideas which eventually developed into Far Eastern Buddhist sects such as Chan and Zen. On the other, they created, over the centuries, disinctive Central Asian forms of Buddhism of which substantial but often uninterpretable traces remain.

The great archaeological expeditions which started in the early twentieth century with the scholarly journeys of Sir Aurel Stein, and which continue today, have done much to reclaim knowledge of a Buddhist world whose material life crumbled under the twin pressures of a ferocious climate and changing political and demographic circumstances, notably the arrival of Islam toward the end of the first millennium CE. Although the desert has obliterated entire towns and monasteries, the arid climate has preserved thousands of manuscripts and inscriptions—from letters, military documents, and trading inventories to complex Buddhist *sutras*—in both sacred and vernacular languages. Today, as these continue to be studied, they reveal a dramatic panorama of life and thought, fascinating in its diversity and fabulous in both color and mystery.

CENTRAL ASIAN BUDDHIST ART

As most profusely demonstrated at Dunhuang, the art of Central Asia developed from the styles taken east by Indian and Gandharan artists. The most impressive remains on the southern route are paintings and sculptures at Khotan in a fluid relaxation of Gandharan style, while ninth-century frescoes in the "Thousand Buddha Caves" at Bezeklik retain something of the hieratic composure of both Gupta and Gandharan idioms. The colossal figures of Vairochana Buddha and Shakyamuni Buddha carved into cliffs at Bamiyan, about 150 miles (240km) from Kabul in Afghanistan, and described by the Chinese monk Xuanzang on his famous pilgrimage of 630CE, were until recently the best preserved expressions of Mahayana devotion to have survived in the Silk Road kingdoms (see page 57). These two Buddhas were destroyed in March 2001 by an intolerant regime, and although there are plans to rebuild them the demolition of the original sculptures represents an incalculable cultural loss.

chapter 3

SRI LANKA AND SOUTHEAST ASIA

THE SOUTHERN TRADITION

OPPOSITE

Part of a scene showing the Buddha mourned by a princess (left), his disciple Ananda (right), and deities. A detail from a gold leaf and black lacquer panel in the Lacquer Pavilion, part of Suan Pakkad palace, Bangkok, Thailand. Dating from the reign of King Narai ("the Great," 1656–88), the wooden panels were originally part of a building in Ayutthaya.

SRI LANKA

ISLAND OF DHARMA

A gilded bronze figure of the meditating Buddha, ca. 800CE. It is 13.5 inches (33.5cm) tall and bears traces of red paint. It was found at Veragala Sirisangabo *vihara* (monastery) at Allavava, near the ancient capital of Anuradhapura. The restrained but sensual style is typical of Sri Lankan images of the Buddha.

Tradition records that Buddhism came to Sri Lanka in the third century BCE from India, as part of the missionary activity of the great Mauryan emperor Ashoka (see pages 42–44). It is said that Ashoka sent his own son, Mahendra (Pali, Mahinda), to the island to convert its ruler, King Devanampiyatissa, an occasion commemorated to this day in Sri Lanka on the popular festival of Poson. Held on the full moon in May or June, the festival attracts Buddhist pilgrims from all over the island to Anuradhapura, the ancient capital, and to Sri Lanka's oldest Buddhist site, Mihintale, eight miles (13km) away, where Mahinda first taught the Dharma.

Anuradhapura became the focus of the Sri Lankan Sangha, which by the third century CE had divided into three broad schools, each centered on a monastery in the capital: the Mahavihara ("Great Monastery"), founded by Mahinda (third century BCE), the Abhayaghirivihara (first century CE), and the Jetavana (third century CE). As elsewhere in the Buddhist world, these divisions should not to be understood as absolute schisms. Nonetheless, there were distinct differences among them, with the Abhayaghirivihara and Jetavana evidently receptive to Mahayana ideas from India, which for a time enjoyed a degree of popularity in Sri Lanka. This is indicated by evidence for the cult of Avalokiteshvara (Lokeshvara) and Tara, *bodhisattva*s of compassion who are widely popular in Mahayana Buddhism.

RIGHT
Solid cast as a single piece, this magnificent 8th-century gilded bronze figure portrays the *bodhisattva* Tara, the female counterpart of Avalokiteshvara, her right hand in the gesture of giving. The goddess, who may once have been inlaid with jewels, is further evidence of the Mahayana in Sri Lanka.

RECORDING THE SCRIPTURES

When Mahinda arrived in Sri Lanka, there were no Buddhist writings. At that period, the discourses and other teachings of the Buddha were memorized and transmitted orally from one generation of teachers to the next. The Dharma was not written down until the first century BCE, when five hundred Sri Lankan *arhats* are said to have assembled at Aluvihara to write down, in Pali (a language closely allied to Sanskrit), the entire teachings of the Buddha and the commentaries upon them. The decision to commit the teachings to writing may have been driven by the pressures of social disruption due to war, and perhaps by the desire of the Mahavihara to uphold its claims to orthodoxy in the face of doctrinal rivalry within the Sangha. Largely through the efforts of the great Indian scholar Buddhaghosa, who organized and translated into Pali the Mahavihara body of Sinhala commentaries in the fourth century CE, the Sri Lankan Pali canon and tradition of written commentary became standard for the Theravada tradition (see page 10), and remain so to this day. Nevertheless, the ability to recite the Buddha's teachings entirely from memory has continued to be valued, particularly in the Theravada tradition.

STATE AND SANGHA

From its very outset, with the conversion of one king by the son of another, Sri Lankan Buddhism was intimately linked to the ruling dynasty, and the Sangha's close relationship with the state has also tradi-tionally characterized other Theravada countries such as Burma and Thailand. In these lands, royal patronage became a key factor in the maintenance and expansion of Buddhist institutions, and a means by

which successive rulers expressed the important Buddhist principles of donation (*dana*) and its attendant virtue of generosity (*shila*). This accounts for the impressive monuments at such sites as the old capital of Anuradhapura and nearby Mihintale, the location of Mahinda's first sermon to King Devanampiyatissa. The ruins of the later capital at Polonnaruwa (ninth century CE onward), showing Mahayana and Hindu influence, are even more elaborate (see illustrations on pages 64 and 65).

All three Sri Lankan schools were founded at royal instigation, and in the twelfth century CE it was another ruler, King Parakramabahu I, who amalgamated the schools under Mahavihara leadership as part of a major reform of the Sangha following a series of devastating invasions from South India. The upheavals of this period also resulted in the end of the Sangha's female lineage of nuns, and the permanent shift in the royal capital from Anuradhapura to Polonnaruwa in the south.

The period of the ninth to the twelfth centuries was a high point in the Buddhist civilization of Sri Lanka, during which the Sangha was a highly privileged group whose leaders had close links to the ruling secular elites. However, further destructive wars and invasions from South India instigated a decline in the fortunes of the Sangha that culminated in the occupation of much of the island by the Portuguese (1505–1658), the Dutch (1658–1796), and the British (1796–1948). At times during this period, the Sangha was forced to seek help from other Theravada states to keep its higher ordination lineages functioning.

Following the fall of the independent kingdom of Kandy to the British in 1815, Sri Lanka came entirely under foreign control. The ancient tradition of state support for the Sangha gave way abruptly to the colonial authority's indifference or outright hostility toward Buddhism, accompanied by the arrival of Christian missionaries. However, from the late nineteenth century, a combination of Westerners interested in Buddhism and Sinhalese Buddhist nationalism stimulated a revival in the Sangha, which was once more flourishing by the time of independence in 1948.

RELICS OF THE BUDDHA

A distinctive aspect of Theravada teaching and art is its emphasis on the exemplary figure of the historical Buddha himself, as well as his previous incarnations as recounted in the *Jataka* stories. Monumental Buddha images are a distinctive feature of Sri Lankan sites, such as the statues carved from a huge granite boulder in Polonnaruwa (see page 65) and other colossal images at Aukana and elsewhere.

The centrality of the Buddha's personal example is reflected in the extraordinary devotion paid to his relics. Ancient Sri Lankan chronicles claim that the Buddha made three journeys to Sri Lanka, stopping at a succession of places later sanctified by enshrined relics, including Mihintale and Sripada (Adam's Peak), where he reputedly left a footprint. Mahinda, in the third century BCE, is said to have sent to India for relics including the Buddha's alms bowl and right collarbone. Later, a hair relic was brought to the island, followed in the fourth century CE by the most famous relic of all, the Buddha's tooth, now preserved at the famous Temple of the Tooth at Kandy and venerated in daily rituals as well as at the annual festival of Esala Perahera.

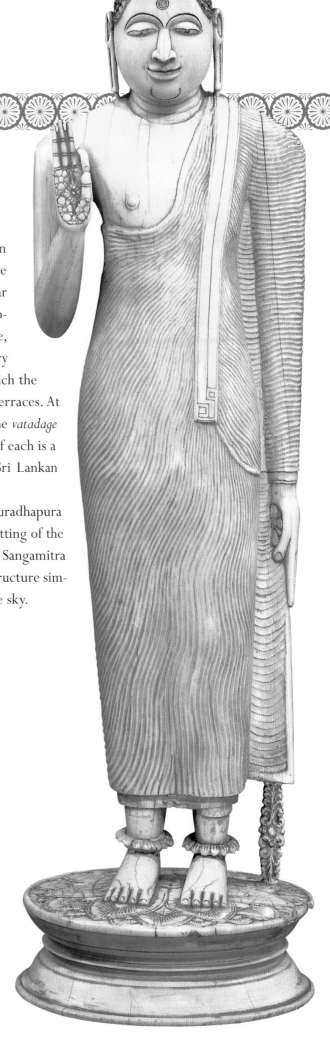

Such relics were housed in stupas, which as at early Indian sites characteristically stand at the center of a monastic complex. The Sri Lankan stupa, or *dagoba*, varies in form but is basically a circular dome-like structure on a square base topped by a conical "spire" (representing umbrellas) rising from its own smaller square-shaped base, or *harmika*. The Ruwanweliseya stupa at Anuradhapura (third century BCE) is a typical example. A striking variation is the *vatadage*, in which the stupa is enclosed within a roofed rotunda at the top of concentric terraces. At Polonnaruwa and nearby Madirigiriya (see pages 34–35 and 64), the *vatadage* has four entranceways oriented to the four directions. At the foot of each is a fine "moonstone," a carved semicircular paving slab common in Sri Lankan architecture; at the top is a seated Buddha.

Another notable variant on the stupa is the structure at Anuradhapura that "houses" the Sri Maha Bodhi, the revered tree grown from a cutting of the original Bodhi tree at Bodh Gaya, brought to the island in 249BCE by Sangamitra (Pali, Sangamitta), Mahinda's sister. Because it is a living tree, the structure simply encloses the ground on which the tree stands and is open to the sky.

OPPOSITE
An 18th-century gilded bronze Buddha standing within a 1-foot (31cm) silver ceremonial arch (a type also found in south India). His right hand is raised in *vitarka mudra*, the gesture of debate or argument. The arch, crowned by an auspicious lion's head, emerges from the jaws of mythical *makara*s (sea monsters).

RIGHT
Ivory figural carving from Kandy, capital (1592–1815) of the last Sri Lankan kingdom, was highly regarded. This 18th-century ivory Buddha shows him wearing a densely pleated robe with the right shoulder bare. The right hand is raised in *vitarka mudra*. The Buddha's palm is adorned with auspicious marks.

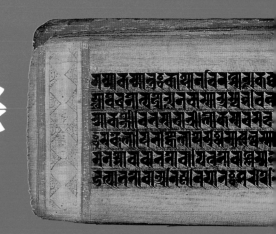

THE ART OF THE BOOK

BELOW
Part of a Pali manuscript in Burmese script on silvered palm leaf with black-lacquered margins. The text is "The Turning of the Wheel of the Dharma," the Buddha's first sermon after his enlightenment, setting out his fundamental teachings, such as the Four Noble Truths (see pages 26–28). The marginal decorations represent the "Wheel of the Dharma," a symbol used in early Buddhist art to represent the Buddha himself. Burma, ca. 1800.

Following the writing down of the Pali canon in Sri Lanka in the first century BCE (see page 63) the copying and distribution of the written Buddhist scriptures became an important and meritorious activity. It was taken up with considerable zeal in Mahayana areas, where there was a particular desire to make the teachings available as widely as possible. The oldest medium used for writing the scriptures were burnished leaves of the fan palm tree, or talipot (*Corypha*), which had long been widely used throughout the Indian subcontinent. The earliest surviving palm leaf manuscripts are Mahayana *Perfection of Wisdom* writings of around the eleventh century. The typical narrow, rectangular shape of the palm-leaf manuscript was carried over into other media, including birchbark, silk, and copper sheets.

Buddhism contributed directly to the success of two Chinese inventions that revolutionized the production and distribution of the scriptures. Paper was invented

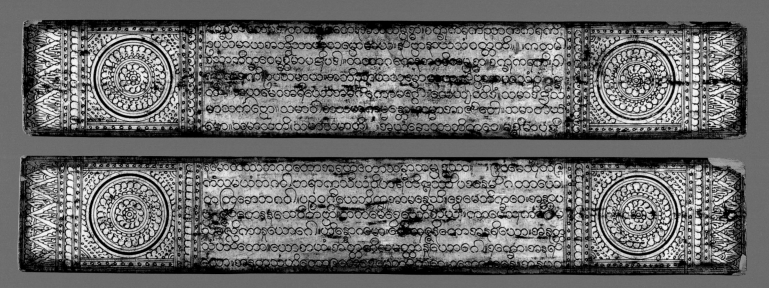

in China in the second century CE, and the earliest surviving Buddhist texts in the new medium date from the following century. During the Tang dynasty (618–906CE), the desire to speed up the dissemination of Buddhist texts led directly to the invention of printing on paper and other media, such as silk, in the seventh century. The oldest extant printed book is a 16-feet-plus (5m) long scroll of the *Diamond Sutra*, which is dated 868CE (see pages 112–113).

As well as the scroll format, concertina-style folded books were also produced, (sometimes also stitched down one side), a form still used in Thailand and Burma. Texts printed from carved woodblocks spread rapidly throughout East Asia, where rulers sponsored editions (in Chinese) of the entire canon printed from tens of thousands of individual blocks. A famous example is at Korea's Haeinsa temple, where the original thirteenth-century woodblocks of the Tripitaka are kept to this day (see pages 139–140).

Paper allowed manuscripts to be a great variety of sizes and formats. However, in Tibet and India Buddhist scriptures continued to employ the traditional horizontal format of palm-leaf and birch-bark manuscripts.

ABOVE

A manuscript from Vikramasila monastery, Bihar, of one of the oldest and most important Mahayana sutras, *The Perfection of Wisdom in 8,000 Verses*, which emerged ca. 1st century CE. The two figures are the *bodhisattvas* Avalokiteshvara (top) and Maitreya, the Buddha of the future. Such manuscripts afford an idea of the riches of Indian Buddhist painting, most of which has been lost. Ink and gouache on palm leaves, ca. 1135.

BURMA

KINGDOMS OF THE IRRAWADDY

BELOW
Siddhartha, the future Buddha, in the palace of his father before he renounced his life of earthly riches to embark on his spiritual quest. A detail of an 18th-century Burmese cotton tapestry.

Like the Sri Lankans, the Burmese have a legend that the Buddha himself visited their land, while ancient Sinhala chronicles claim that the Emperor Ashoka sent a Buddhist mission to the land of "Suwarnabhumi" in the third century BCE. This was possibly the kingdom of the Mons, based on Thaton in Lower Burma and stretching into what is now Thailand. Whatever the truth of the legend and the chronicles, the Mon kingdom seems to have come under the cultural influence of northern India at an early period, with forms of Buddhism, as well as Hinduism, established in Lower Burma by the early centuries CE.

Evidence points to the Mons converting fully to Buddhism only around the fifth century CE: the earliest evidence of Theravada Buddhism in southeast Asia is a

series of Pali inscriptions from the Mon kingdom dating from around this time. The great age of Mon civilization was from the sixth to the eleventh centuries, centered on the Dvaravati kingdom in Lower Burma and Thailand (see pages 76–79).

While the Mons dominated Lower Burma, Tibeto-Burmese peoples of the far eastern Himalayas founded states in the north, center, and southwest of present-day Burma. Some of these peoples, such as the Pyu of central Burma, followed Mahayana and Tantric Buddhism as well as Theravada and Hindu practices. It was from one of these migrant mountain peoples—the Bamar, or Myanma—that Burma (Myanmar) takes its name. According to tradition the Myanma founded their capital, Pagan, on the great Irrawaddy (Ayeyarwaddy) River in 849CE.

THE GOLDEN AGE OF PAGAN

The Pagan kingdom (1044–1287) attained supremacy in Burma in the eleventh century under the remarkable King Anawrahta or Anuruddha (1044–77). Said to have been converted to Theravada Buddhism by a Mon monk, Anawrahta forged links with the Sri Lankan Sangha and firmly established Theravada as his kingdom's—and subsequently the region's—dominant form of Buddhism. The climax of Anawrahta's reign came in 1057, when he captured the Mon city of Thaton and removed its ruler, together with many Theravada monks and craftsmen, to Pagan. From this point, the number of Mahayana and Tantric practitioners rapidly diminished, as the Theravada

ABOVE

Dating to the 15th century or later, this ceramic tile depicts ass-headed warriors of Mara, the demon who tempted the Buddha as he approached enlightenment. They are similar to those that adorn buildings commemorating the first seven weeks of the Buddha's enlightenment built by King Dhammaceti (1472–92) close to Shwegugyi pagoda, near Pegu. Rows of glazed pottery tiles were a feature of Burmese temples from the Pagan period onward.

LEFT
Serenity and power are combined in the classic Burmese image of the Buddha calling the earth to witness his enlightenment. This 20th-century brass statue from the Shwedagon pagoda is in the so-called "Mandalay" style, with a wide fillet band around the forehead and thickly folded robes.

flourished under the patronage of the Pagan kings. As in Sri Lanka, such state patronage of the Sangha became a key aspect of Burmese Buddhism, and this is reflected in the astonishing assemblage of monuments constructed at royal behest at Pagan (see pages 78–81).

Anawrahta forged close links with the Sri Lankan ruler Vijayabahu I, and the two monarchs sent one another relics and scriptures and even monastic personnel. Sri Lanka's Mahavihara lineage came to prominence in Burma through the influence of Sri Lankan-trained monks. In return the Burmese Sangha helped Vijayabahu to restore the Sri Lankan ordination lineage following devastating invasions from southern India. Vijayabahu's gratitude was expressed by the gift of a copy of the famous relic of the Buddha's tooth, subsequently enshrined in Pagan's magnificent Shwezigon Paya (see page 78).

It was in this period that the distinctive forms of Burmese art arose, under the influence of Mon styles. As in other Theravada traditions, the figure of the Buddha dominated as the subject of large and small statuary. Burmese artists achieved a distinctive expressive beauty in what was a far narrower range of subject matter than that found in Mahayana traditions. Like the Mons, they (and their monastic and royal patrons) demonstrated a particular fondness for images of the Buddha on the point of his awakening, touching the ground to call the earth to witness to his enlightenment, signaling the defeat of the demon Mara. In Burmese representations of the subject, the gesture of touching of the ground (Sanskrit, *bhumisparsha mudra*) is often emphasized by showing the Buddha leaning forward slightly, lending the image a powerful sense of

ABOVE
Towering some 320 feet (98m) above a forest of smaller shrines to *nats*, or nature spirits, Rangoon's famous Shwedagon pagoda is one of the finest examples of the typical Burmese stupa, which blends the stepped base, dome, and spire of the Indian and Sri Lankan stupa into an elegantly tapering whole. Its current form probably dates from ca. 1400.

movement that highlights the significance of what was, after all, the most momentous event in the Buddha's life.

The characteristic Burmese stupa or pagoda (*zedi*) also developed at this time. Taking the tall spire and square terraced base of the Mon stupa, the Burmese *zedi* evolved elegant, fluid lines that played down the distinctive individual elements of the traditional Indian and Sri Lankan stupa from which it was ultimately derived. In this scheme, the square *harmika*, from which the spire emerges in the Indian-Sri Lankan model, does not appear, while the spire itself continues the tapering, bell-like profile of the main structure.

DISUNITY AND REVIVAL

The Pagan kingdom was destroyed by the Mongols in 1257, and a period of political fragmentation followed, with the Shans, an ethnically Thai people, dominating the north and the Mons regaining independence in the south. The culture of Pagan underwent a revival in the Burmese kingdom centered on Ava (Inwa) on the Irrawaddy, founded in the mid-fourteenth century. Perhaps as a result of Mahayana influence, the repertoire of Buddha iconography was expanded in this century by images of the Buddha richly adorned in the royal crown and regalia of a *chakravartin*, or universal ruler.

In the south, the independent Mon state that arose in the fifteenth century at Pegu witnessed a brief flourishing before it fell a century later to

a revitalized Myanma state centered on Toungoo, which also captured the Shan regions of the north. The Toungoo dynasty (1531–1752) and the succeeding Konbaung dynasty (1753–1885) became embroiled in a prolonged conflict with the neighboring Thai kingdom of Ayutthaya, which was eventually defeated in 1767. The Konbaung dynasty's conquest of Assam in 1824 triggered the three Anglo-Burmese wars that finally saw all of Burma incorporated into British India in 1885. However, the latter decades of Burmese independence also witnessed a flourishing of Buddhism. The peaceable King Mindon (1853–78), who convened the Fifth Buddhist Council in 1871, also left a remarkable monument in the form of the entire Theravada scriptures engraved on more than seven hundred marble tablets at Mandalay's Kuthodaw pagoda.

As in Sri Lanka, colonial rule severed the traditional link between the state and the Sangha, which Burmese kings had directly controlled through the appointment of a head cleric, the Sangharaja ("Sangha King") or Thathanabaing. This office lapsed under British rule, but Buddhism itself continued to flourish, and does so to this day. Renewed official patronage (and attempted control) of the Sangha since independence in 1947 has at times, particularly in recent decades, placed Burmese Buddhists in an awkward and even perilous position. However, monks continue to perform their daily alms rounds, important ancient temples and pagodas are magnificently (if sometimes controversially) maintained, and the status of Buddhism as the basis of the nation's traditional culture remains unquestioned.

ABOVE

In 1871 King Mindon convened a council at Mandalay in Upper Burma, the capital of the last Burmese kingdom, to establish a definitive text of the Theravada Buddhist canon, the Pali *Tipitaka*. The texts were then inscribed on 729 marble tablets, which were housed in the many smaller shrines shown here surrounding Mandalay's gilded Kuthodaw pagoda, built by Mindon in 1857.

PAGAN

CITY OF GOLDEN SHRINES

ABOVE
Located 4 miles (7km) northeast of the old walled core of Pagan, the Shwezigon Paya (built 1059–1090) still retains its basic 11th-century form, which served as a model for stupas all over Burma.

OPPOSITE AND RIGHT
The Ananda (built ca. 1105), one of the largest temples at Pagan (see page 80). Laid out in an equal-armed cruciform plan (right), each arm forms a hall that leads to the central shrine.

Owing to a strong Burmese Buddhist tradition that founding a new temple earns more merit than maintaining an old one, Burma has more temples and pagodas (stupas) than any other country in the Buddhist world. Nowhere is this more evident than at the medieval capital of Pagan (Bagan). Long after its royal palaces and other wooden buildings have disappeared, the sheer number of surviving buildings in more durable materials is astonishing. Within an area covering around 25 square miles (65 sq km), there are more than 900 temples, 500 pagodas (*paya* or *zedi*), and 400 monasteries, together with the remains of hundreds of other sacred sites.

Founded in the mid-ninth century on a bend in the Irrawaddy (Ayeyarwaddy) River in Burma's dry central region, Pagan was the capital of a kingdom that governed much of present-day Burma and beyond until its fall to the Mongols in 1257. Even though the city thereafter declined in political importance, its great shrines such as the Shwezigon and the Ananda retained their religious significance and attract pilgrims from all over the country to the present day.

Pagan reached its zenith under King Anawrahta (1044–77; see page 73–75) and his successors. Following his conversion to Theravada Buddhism, Anawrahta founded five stupas to delineate the four corners of the city and its symbolic center. The northernmost stupa, the Shwezigon Paya, was planned as a great shrine for important relics of the Buddha, including a part of his collarbone and frontal bone, as well as a replica of the Buddha's tooth that was the gift of the king of Sri Lanka. By the time of his death, Anawrahta had constructed only the lower terraces, which are adorned with carved scenes from the Buddha's previous lives (*jatakas*) and were also remarkable

for the depiction of the thirty-seven *nats*, pre-Buddhist spirits that remain the object of popular devotion among Burmese Buddhists. (The *nats* were later removed from the exterior to a separate building.) The great bell-shaped spire was completed in 1090 by King Kyanzittha (1084–1113). Like many of Pagan's important shrines, the Shwezigon was badly damaged in the 1975 earthquake, but was subsequently carefully repaired and gilded.

THE CITY OF FOUR MILLION PAGODAS

Kyanzittha was such an active and prolific builder of sacred monuments that he earned Pagan the nickname "City of Four Million Pagodas". As well as completing the construction of the Shwezigon, he was also responsible for founding temples, including the Abeyadana, the Nagayon, and above all the Ananda (see plan and illustration on pages 78–79). Pagan's most important temple, and perhaps the only Burmese temple in constant use since its construction, the Ananda is built on a four-armed cross-shaped ground plan . It consists of four large halls around a central shrine area, which is marked by a soaring 170-foot (52m) tower in a "beehive" style reminiscent of an Indian temple. The Ananda, like the Shwezigon, is built of small stone blocks or bricks stuccoed to resemble stonework. The soft stucco allowed Burmese artists to adorn the temple with elaborate sculptural ornament, a feature that distinguishes Burmese temples and pagodas.

THAILAND

PRINCES OF THE SANGHA

The recorded history of Thailand begins with the establishment of the civilization of the Mons by the fifth century CE. The Mons were closely related to the Khmers and it is believed that both peoples migrated from the area of southern China into Southeast Asia ca. 850BCE. The Khmers settled along the valley of the lower Mekong River, while the Mon settled in the highlands and central plains of present-day Thailand as well as in modern Burma.

The Mon Dvaravati civilization, which dominated the region from the sixth to the eleventh centuries, seems to have comprised a kingdom or kingdoms with its major cultural centers on or near the Chao Phraya River in central Thailand. These centers included Nakorn Pathom, Dvaravati, and Lvo (Lopburi) as well as U Thong, Khu Bua, and Si Thep. Other important Mon cities were Haripunjaya in northern Thailand and Thaton in present-day Lower Burma. The oldest extant inscription in Mon, a language related to Khmer and Vietnamese, dates to ca. 600CE and was discovered near Thailand's tallest sacred structure, the Nakorn Pathom stupa, 40 miles (64km) from the present-day capital Bangkok.

The Mons appear to have adopted Theravada Buddhism by the sixth century, but it is also clear from archaeological evidence that although Theravada was the dominant religion, Mahayana Buddhism was present among the Mon, as also was Hinduism—as shown by depictions of popular Hindu deities such as Vishnu and Brahma.

THE ART OF DVARAVATI

Dvaravati buildings were largely of wood and therefore few have survived apart from the remains of brick-built stupas

OPPOSITE

The Buddha protected by the
multi-headed *naga* (serpent deity)
Muchalinda. According to
legend, the god sheltered the
Buddha during a storm as he
meditated under the Bodhi Tree
following his enlightenment. A
stone sculpture from the former
Thai royal capital of Ayutthaya.

RIGHT

A 14th-century bronze from the
Sukhotai period of the Buddha
walking with his right hand in
"fear-allaying" gesture (*abhaya
mudra*). Most Buddha images in
Asia show him standing, sitting,
or lying; the "walking Buddha"
is a distinctive creation of Thai
art (see also page 86).

(called *chedi* in Thailand) and temples, many of which were much rebuilt over the centuries. Stupa remains show the tall spires and square, terraced bases that are found in the later, Mon-influenced, architecture of the Burmese kingdom of Pagan. Like the Pagan examples, Mon stupas were decorated with stucco and stone carvings, as well as arrays of niches on the lower terraces that were filled with sculptures. Mon stone temples, also like those of Pagan and other Burmese sites, seem to have been derived from Hindu models, with an essentially square base and pyramid-shaped roof.

Perhaps the very first Buddhist images in Southeast Asia were those produced by the Dvaravati culture. As elsewhere in the Theravada world, the favored subject for Dvaravati artists was the Buddha himself. The Buddha is depicted sitting in meditation both before his enlightenment, and also a short time afterward, when he is shown being protected by the giant snake-deity Muchalinda— a subject that appealed to Buddhists in the snake-infested regions of Southeast Asia. Together with standing images of the Buddha in the posture of teaching (a probable reference to his first sermon at Sarnath following his enlightenment), such Dvaravati images reveal many of the stylistic influences of Gupta India (see pages 50–55).

Mon supremacy ended with the occupation of much of central Thailand by the Khmer kingdom under King Suryavarman of Angkor (1010–50CE), and the defeat of the Mons of Tathom by Anawrahta of Pagan in 1057 (see page 73). In the former Mon areas of central and western Thailand, the Khmers dominated until about 1260, which probably accounts for the reemergence at this time of strong Hindu and

Mahayana influences alongside the Theravada. There is sculptural evidence that the Mahayana *bodhisattvas* Avalokiteshvara and Maitreya (the messianic Buddha of the future) were popular in western Thailand in this period.

LORDS OF SUKHOTAI AND AYUTTHAYA

During the Khmer period new migrants arrived in the area from southern China: the Thais, who established powerful kingdoms from the thirteenth century, most notably those centered on Sukhotai (ca.1240–1438) and Chiangmai (1296–1599) in the north and Ayutthaya (or Ayudhya, 1350–1767) and finally Bangkok (1767–present) in the south. In ca. 1260 Sukhotai wrested its independence from the Khmers, and Theravada Buddhism was subsequently affirmed as the kingdom's state religion by King Rama Khamheng (1275–1317) and by his grandson, Lü Thai (1340–61), who invited learned Sri Lankan monks to the kingdom (and eventually abdicated to become a monk himself).

As in Sri Lanka and Burma, the organization of the Sangha in the Thai kingdoms became intimately connected to royal influence and patronage; unlike these two countries, however, the link has continued unbroken to the present day, because Thailand was alone in Southeast Asia in remaining free of European colonialism. Since 1902 the Thai Sangha has had a hierarchy of offices parallel to that of the secular state; at the head is the Supreme Patriarch, who is appointed by the king.

A distinctive Thai style of art began to emerge from its Dvaravati and Khmer antecedents in the thirteenth century. The seated Buddha, for example, acquired a refined, almost abstract stylization and fluidity that emphasized the spiritual power of

ABOVE
Wat Chai Wattanaram, one of the most impressive temple remains of the old capital of Ayutthaya. It was built by the tyrannical King Prasat Tong (1629–56), perhaps to assert his legitimacy as ruler; he was a commoner who had deposed his predecessor. It has a central Khmer-style *prang* (tower), representing Mount Meru, surrounded by smaller towers. Sacked in 1767, the temple has been partly restored.

OPPOSITE
The Buddha calling the earth to witness his enlightenment. This is the most frequent Thai image of the Buddha, but twin statues such as these in Wat Boworniwet temple, Bangkok, are unusual. The front statue is more than 600 years old. The seat of the Thai Sangha's Supreme Patriarch, this temple is also where recent kings have been ordained as monks.

Wat Pho, Bangkok's oldest and largest temple, dates from 200 years before the city became the Thai capital. It was remodeled in the ornate post-Ayutthaya style by kings Rama I and III. The temple houses a huge reclining Buddha 153 feet (46m) long and 50 feet (15m) high, and in the grounds stand hundreds of Buddha statues, many from Ayutthaya and other places sacked by the Burmese.

OPPOSITE
A head of the Buddha with the elongated ears and decorated crown typical of the Ayutthaya period. A further characteristic of Thai Buddha images is the prominent flame-like *ushnisha* or "wisdom bump" on the crown of the head. Bronze, ca. 1500.

the subject as he touched the ground in token of his final victory over the demon Mara. As if to emphasize this further, the Buddha is depicted with a flame emerging from his *ushnisha* or "wisdom bump."

The elegance and elongated features that characterize such images are evident in Sukhotai depictions of the Buddha walking. Unique in Asian Buddhist art, the Thai "walking Buddha" image effortlessly combines grace with dynamism in a potent image of the vitality of the Dhamma (Dharma), and of the humanness and accessibility of the Buddha. Like the seated Buddha, such figures were often carved in stone, though bronze became popular (see page 83).

THAI SACRED ARCHITECTURE

Unfortunately much Thai architecture from before the late eighteenth century was damaged or destroyed in a devastating series of wars between the Ayutthaya kingdom and the Burmese, which culminated in the sack of Ayutthaya in 1767. However, from what remains or has been reconstructed it is clear that the rulers of Sukhotai and their cultural heirs in Ayutthaya were influenced by Dvaravati and Khmer styles in their use of stuccoed brick and exterior decorative elements. Sri Lankan influence was also evident following the strong ties established with Sri Lankan Sangha by the Sukhotai rulers. However, one distinctive feature to evolve at Sukhotai was the *poom khao bin*, or "lotus-bud" profile of the Thai *chedi* (stupa). Following the fall of Ayutthaya and the move first to Thonburi on the Chao Phraya River and then—under King Rama I (1782–1809), founder of the current Chakri dynasty—across the river to Ratanakosin (Bangkok), new building styles emerged. They did not differ greatly in external form from their predecessors, but were marked by more intricate and delicate decoration, under the influence of Chinese architecture.

THAI PAINTING

COLORS OF ENLIGHTENMENT

Traditional Thai artists composed their work by first assigning the principal scenes to particular areas of the painting. These key areas were then isolated from the rest of the composition by borders that dispensed with the need for perspective—rather like in medieval European sacred art, the size of a figure reflected its importance, not its position in the landscape. Figures were drawn in two dimensions, without shading, and landscapes were rarely atmospheric, serving principally as neutral stage scenery against which the main scenes were played out. These were painted in a delicate and subtle tempera palette comprising five main colors (white, black, blue, red, and yellow).

Within these conventions, traditional artists produced exquisite works in the form of cloth banners, manuscript illustrations, and temple wall paintings. Thai murals are primarily instructional, intended to convey clear moral values in straightforward and direct images. As in other Theravada lands, favored themes were episodes from the Buddha's life as well as *Jataka* stories. Other subjects include depictions of deities, heavens, and hells. Unfortunately, painting of the pre-Bangkok period suffered great loss and damage during the Burmese wars of the eighteenth century. Apart from a few remaining murals—most were destroyed along with the temples and palaces they adorned—the glories of Thai painting before the fall of the kingdom of Ayutthaya in 1767 are glimpsed principally through manuscripts. But even mural paintings executed after this period have proved vulnerable, since tempera on plaster is very susceptible to moisture damage in the damp, humid climate.

Following the reestablishment of Thai independence after 1767 and the founding of a new capital at Bangkok, traditional Thai painting evolved as a result of contacts with China, which led to the import of Chinese pigments, and with Europe, which saw the introduction of chemical paints and the use of perspective. The result was a strikingly richer and bolder palette that might also use copious gold leaf to fill formerly neutral intermediate or background areas.

CAMBODIA AND LAOS

KINGDOMS OF THE MEKONG

From the ninth to the fifteenth centuries, much of Southeast Asia was dominated by the Khmers, who ruled from their great capital of Angkor in the valley of the Mekong River. At their height of influence, the Khmers—a people ethnically related to the Mons of Thailand and Burma—held sway over an area that encompassed present-day Cambodia and much of Thailand. Established by King Jayavarman II in 802 CE, the Khmer kingdom reached its peak after the tenth century; the end of Khmer supremacy was marked by the abandonment of Angkor in 1432, during a series of conflicts with the Thais. From that time Khmer kings ruled a much reduced state from a new capital at Phnom Penh. However, notwithstanding the decline of Khmer power, and the subsequent Thai political domination of the Khmers until the late eighteenth century, the influence of Khmer culture remained strong throughout the region.

Under the cultural influence of northen India, the Khmer kings embraced Hinduism, but many also supported Buddhism, and the monuments and artworks that resulted from Khmer royal patronage are some of the greatest in the Buddhist world. Most kings followed a strand of Mahayana Buddhism that developed in India and was much influenced by Hindu forms, both in its rituals and monuments. Sanskrit was the language of religion and officialdom, as shown by the Sanskrit names taken by Khmer rulers. Theravada Buddhism seems to have arrived rather later among the Khmers than elsewhere in Southeast Asia, with the earliest Theravada inscription, in a private shrine, dated no earlier than ca. 1230. The first ruler fully to embrace Theravada was Jayavarman Parameshvara (1327–?1353?), by whose reign the Khmer kingdom was past its zenith. Since that period, Theravada Buddhism—which was probably promoted by contacts with the Thai Sangha—has been the principal religion of Cambodians.

THE GOD-KINGS OF ANGKOR
A striking feature of Khmer civilization was its cult of the *devaraja*, or divine monarch, a concept that may go back to the Hindu rulers of Funan (1st–7th centuries CE) and

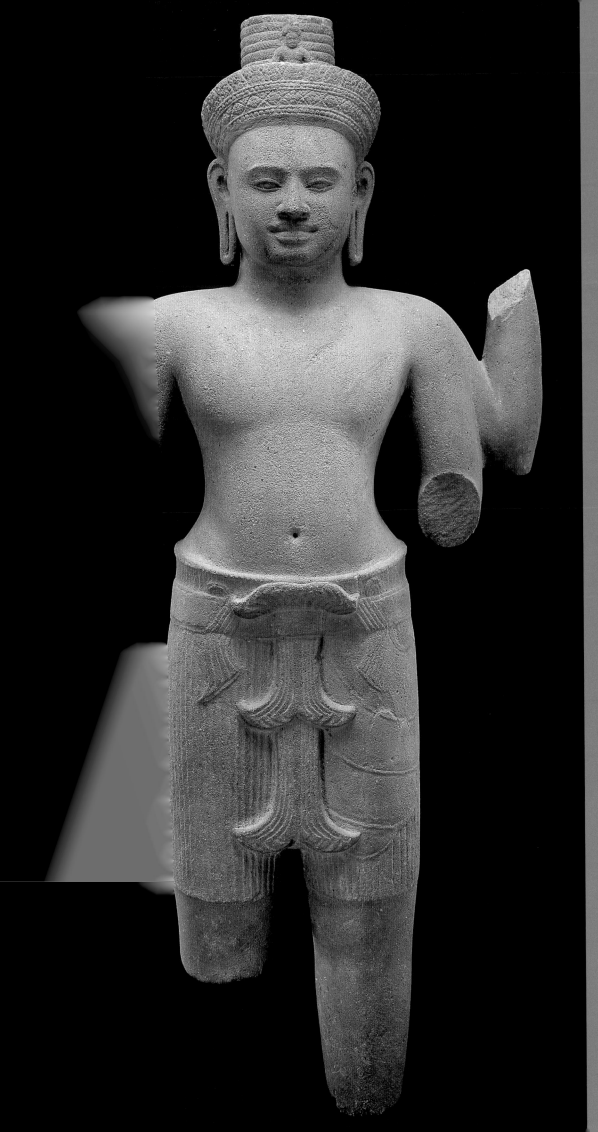

Avalokiteshvara, (Lokeshvara), the lord of compassion, is the most popular *bodhisattva* among the Khmers. He is represented as multiarmed, eternally ready to assist suffering humanity. In the topknot of the *bodhisattva's* stylized coiffure is an image of the celestial Buddha Amitabha, "Infinite Radiance," of whom Lokeshvara is believed to be an emanation. This powerfully expressive sandstone statue is in the relatively unadorned pre-Angkorian Khleang style, dating to the late 10th century.

Zhenla (7th–9th centuries CE), the states that preceded the first independent Khmer kingdom. Alongside the array of Hindu and Buddhist deities adorning the astonishing monuments of Angkor appear images of the king as a kind of god or *bodhisattva*—quite literally in the case of Jayavarman II, whose sculpted features strikingly resemble those of Avalokiteshvara (Lokeshvara), the *bodhisattva* of infinite compassion. This royal self-image is probably also seen on the Buddha statue erected by Jayavarman VII at the heart of Angkor's Bayon temple, and on its famous four-faced towers (see pages 96–99).

Jayavarman VII (ruled 1181–1219) is renowned among Khmer monarchs as the greatest builder of Buddhist monuments, as seen at Angkor and at such other temples as Ta Prohm, south of Phnom Penh, which is noted for its fine reliefs. It is typical of the syncretic tendencies of Khmer religion that even this Buddhist monarch dedicated Ta Prohm to both the Buddha and the Hindu god Brahma; he also gave Shiva and Vishnu their own shrines at the Bayon and elsewhere.

Khmer Buddhist architecture differs strikingly from that of Thailand or Burma in its general absence of the stupa as a separate monumental structure. Following

Hindu models, Khmer temples were designed in the form of a great temple-mountain representing Mount Meru, the center of the universe in the cosmology of both Hindus and Buddhists. Within the precincts of a Khmer temple there might be small devotional stupas, but the overall scheme of the temple left little room, literally and figuratively, for soaring monumental pagodas of the type seen at Pagan or Ayutthaya.

Khmer temples were built on a quadrilateral plan, oriented to the four directions and entered through richly decorated monumental doorways. Many, such as the Hindu Angkor Wat and the Buddhist Bayon, had five towers representing the five peaks of Mount Meru. Temples were also surrounded by a moat to emphasize the distinction between earthly and sacred space. Serpent deities, or *nagas*—symbols of the connection between earth and the celestial realm—are common decorative motifs on the bridges or causeways across these temple moats. This feature also alludes to the Hindu creation myth in which divine beings coiled a great serpent around a mountain and, pulling on the serpent's head and tail, turned the mountain to churn the primordial ocean of milk, thus initiating the creation of the universe.

ABOVE

A section of the 1,000 feet (300m) long Terrace of the Elephants at Angkor Thom. Carved along its entire length with elephants, lions, and mythical garudas, the nine feet (2.5m) high stone terrace was built by King Jayavarman VII, probably as a base for audience pavilions and viewing platforms.

LAOS: LAND OF THE GOLDEN BUDDHA

Jayavarman Pareshvara, the first Khmer king to embrace Theravada Buddhism, also played a part in the adoption of Buddhism by Cambodia's northern neighbor, Laos. The various Lao states were united ca. 1350 under Jayavarman's probable son-in-law, King Fa Ngum, who received a delegation of Theravada monks from the Khmer king. As well as the Pali scriptures, the monks brought Fa Ngum a golden statue of the Buddha known as the Phrabang, which gave its name to Fa Ngum's capital, Luang Phrabang ("Shrine of the Phrabang") on the northern Laotian reaches of the Mekong. Both culturally and politically Fa Ngum modeled his kingdom and capital along Khmer lines. Many of Luang Phrabang's finest Buddhist works of art date to the reign of King Visun (1501–20), who completed a program of reconstruction following the city's sack by the Vietnamese in 1479.

From the outset Laos was surrounded by more powerful neighbors, but the kingdom survived by making alliances, not always willingly, variously with the Burmese, Thais, and Vietnamese. Under Thai pressure, King Setthathirat (1548–71) moved the seat of the kingdom south from Luang Phrabang to the present capital of Vien Chan (Vientiane), lower down the Mekong and closer to the Thai city of Ayutthaya. Vien Chan still retains some of Setthathirat's monuments, such as parts of the Khmer-style mountain-temple of Wat That Luang and also the Ho Phra Keo, originally built on the site of a royal palace to house a famous statue known as the "Emerald Buddha." According to legend this image, actually carved from a type of jade—was fashioned by the gods over two thousand years ago, but it was first discovered in the fifteenth century in northern Thailand and taken to Laos in 1551. In 1778 the statue was captured by the Thais and permanently installed in Bangkok's Wat Phra Keo (Temple of the Emerald Buddha), where it is revered to this day as Thailand's most sacred Buddha image.

ABOVE

The Ho Phra Keo (Temple of the Emerald Buddha), was originally built in 1565 by King Setthathirat on the site of the former royal palace at Vien Chan. Largely destroyed by the Thais in 1828, the temple was reconstructed between 1936 and 1942. Today it holds many fine examples of Laotian art, such as these sculptures of the Buddha calling the earth to witness his enlightenment and victory over Mara.

OPPOSITE

A detail of the finely carved and gilded central doors of Wat Mai ("New Monastery"), Luang Prabang. Founded by King Anurat (1795–1819), the *wat* served as the chapel for Laotian royalty and is the seat of the Pra Sangkharat, the head of the Laotian Sangha. For decades it also housed the sacred golden Buddha statue, the Phrabang (see main text).

ANGKOR THOM

TEMPLE OF THE GOD-KING

The ancient complex of Angkor, site of successive royal capitals of the Khmer empire over six centuries, covers a vast area of almost twenty miles by ten miles (32km by 16km) on the northern shores of Cambodia's Great Lake. In a region of abundant water, rice, and fish, Angkor was perfectly suited for the Khmer imperial center. The first royal capital at the site was established in 889 by King Yasovarman I. It was a little over a century later that Suryavarman I (1002–1049) founded the massive complex of Angkor Thom, the "Great City," which was to remain the seat of Khmer kings throughout the period of Khmer imperial greatness.

In its present form, Angkor Thom is effectively two cities fused together. The first was centered on the temple in the royal palace of Suryavarman I. This city was superseded by the one built by Jayavarman VII (1181–1220), a fervent follower of Mahayana Buddhism, who constructed most of the Angkor Thom we see today, as well as the nearby Preah Khan temple and Ta Prohm monasteries. He shifted the nucleus of the city 1,600 feet (500m) southward, building the great Bayon temple at the center of a square-plan capital surrounded by a moat three hundred feet (90m) wide and ten miles (16km) long. The site is a mile (0.6km) to the north of Suryavarman II's (1113–50) great Hindu temple and mausoleum of Angkor Wat.

BELOW
A row of sculpted garudas form part of the so-called Terrace of the Elephants at Angkor Thom (see also illustration on page 93). Of Hindu origin, the mythical serpent-eating garuda is a popular figure in Southeast Asian tradition, usually represented as part human and part eagle.

THE COSMIC TEMPLE

The Bayon follows Khmer temple tradition in its central tower surrounded by four smaller ones, representing Meru, the five-peaked cosmic mountain. The temple, like the city, is oriented to the four directions, and is in effect a massive comsic diagram, or *mandala*. Khmer royal tradition of the ruler as *devaraja*, or god-king, some kind of *bodhisattva*-like world-savior or universal sovereign (*chakravartin*) seems to have been taken one step further by Jayavarman VII when he constructed the Bayon. At the center of the temple stood a statue of the Buddha in the

The north gate of the Bayon (see plan, left), has distinctive towers of carved sandstone which, like most of the temple's 54 towers, bear faces of the *bodhisattva* Lokeshvara (Avalokiteshvara). The temple dates from the reign of Jayavarman VII and its huge, imposing faces are believed to be portraits of Jayavarman himself. In his time, much of the building would have been brightly painted and gilded.

ABOVE, LEFT AND RIGHT
Superb reliefs of royal figures
and deities on the Terrace of the
Leprous King at Angkor Thom.
The terrrace may have been a
royal cremation ground, or
perhaps commemorates a Khmer
king who died of leprosy.

OPPOSITE
A relief from the Bayon depicting
dancing figures of *apsaras,* divine
nymphs who entertain the gods
and become the celestial wives of
kings and heroes who die bravely.

regalia of the *chakrvartin* and with facial features that appear to be a portrait of the
king. Elsewhere, the colossal face of the *bodhisattva* Avalokiteshvara (Lokeshvara), lord
of limitless compassion, presides benignly from the temple's entrance towers over a
host of gods and humans, depicted in sometimes exquisite relief carvings. As with the
temple Buddha, the features of the *bodhisattva* are, most likely, those of Jayavarman VII
himself. These faces are among the most haunting images of Bayon, and like much of
the temple may once have been decorated with paint and gold leaf.

Jayavarman VII's fervor for Buddhism prompted a pro-Hindu backlash in succeeding reigns. Major additions and modifications were made to Angkor Thom by
Jayavarman VIII (1243–1295), notably the obliteration of overtly Buddhist images. All
over the temple, images of the Buddha have been deliberately obliterated or obscured
behind later structures. An exception are the faces on the towers, perhaps out of
respect for what were considered to be royal portraits, or because their Buddhist features were no longer immediately apparent.

INDONESIA AND MALAYSIA

MOUNTAINS OF THE GODS

BELOW

A detail of a Buddha statue in the Burmese Wat Dhammikarama temple, in Georgetown, Penang, Malaysia. Since the arrival of Islam, Buddhism in Malaysia and Indonesia has chiefly been practiced by those of Chinese, Sri Lankan, Burmese, and Thai origin. Malaysia's oldest Burmese temple, Wat Dhammikarama was originally founded in 1803.

As in other parts of Southeast Asia, the spread of Buddhism in Java and Sumatra was shaped by contacts with India. According to tradition, an Indian Buddhist monk landed in a central Javanese kingdom in the fifth century CE and converted the local queen to Buddhism. Under her patronage and that of her son Mahayana Buddhism took root, and contact with northeastern India also ensured that Tantra (Vajryayana) was also present in Java by the year 800.

Vajrayana temples, including Chandi Sewu on Java, became famous throughout the region and Javanese and Sumatran sites were visited by pilgrims from far and wide, such as the Chinese scholars Xuanzang and Yijing, in the seventh century. Yijing studied at Palembang, the capital of Sumatra's Shrivijaya kingdom, an important center of Buddhist learning. Unfortunately, virtually nothing survives from the Shrivijaya period, since most of their temples and other monuments were built of wood.

The Shailendra kingdom on neighboring Java was roughly contemporary with the Shrivijaya. Under the Shailendra, who practiced a syncretic mix of Hinduism and Buddhism, Mahayana Buddhism reached its apogee on the island, from the mid-eighth to mid-tenth centuries. At its height the Shailendra state ruled an empire that included Sumatra, the Malay Peninsula, and as far north as southern Cambodia. It was in this period that the Shailendra kings built on Java one of the most extraordinary Buddhist monuments in the world, the Borobudur (see pages 102–105). Other monuments of this period show the influence of the Gupta style of India. By the year 1100 the Shailendra had shifted their

ABOVE

A Javanese pectoral of embossed gold in the form of a flower with turtles on each petal. In the center is a head of the Buddha. According to the Mahayana *Lotus Sutra*, encountering a Buddha is as rare as the flowering of the udumbara tree (*Ficus glomerata*) or a blind turtle finding a piece of wood in the sea. Buddhist period, pre-1300.

power base from the center of Java to the east, and Hinduism had reemerged as the dominant strand in Javanese religion. Islam arrived in Sumatra by 1300 and within two centuries the majority of the peoples of Sumatra, Java, and the Malay Peninsula had converted, leaving Hinduism to one small enclave, the island of Bali. In these regions today Buddhism is practiced mainly by people of Chinese and Sri Lankan descent, whose ancestors arrived in the nineteenth century.

BOROBUDUR

THE ASCENT OF THE BUDDHA

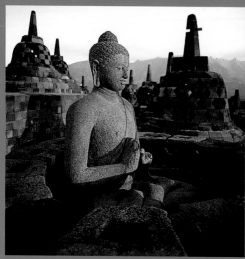

Constructed by the Shailendra kings of central Java (see page 100) around the turn of the ninth century CE, Borobudur ranks with Pagan and Angkor as one of the greatest Buddhist sites in Southeast Asia, although in form and sheer size there is nothing remotely like it anywhere else. Built on a square plan with sides 370 feet (112m) long oriented to the four directions, and rising in nine separate levels to the single stupa-like structure at its peak, Borobudur incorporates nearly two million stone blocks, with 1,500 carved narrative panels; 1,200 decorative panels; more than 500 Buddha images (including 72 inside "miniature stupas" on the upper three terraces); and a further 1,500 or so stupa-shaped decorative elements.

It is uncertain why Borobudur was built and whether it was intended as a temple, a memorial or funerary monument, a gigantic *mandala* (cosmic diagram), or a sort of immense stupa. Possibly it is a combination of both of the latter: as a stupa it would represent the entirety of the Buddha's teaching, the Dharma; and as a *mandala*, the universe in which the Dharma is played out.

No single explanation has clarified the wealth of imagery, but, structurally and iconographically, it is evidently divided into three parts, and according to one theory these represent the three worlds through which one ascends on the path to awakening or enlightenment. The bottom terrace represents the earthly world of *samsara* and perpetual rebirth (see page 26), and is adorned with reliefs depicting the effects of *karma*; this level was later concealed behind stone panels, possibly to shore up the whole structure as it rose.

The central, square-plan, terraces are said to represent the celestial world, the world of the *bodhisattva*, the devotee committed to

the spiritual path. These terraces include the majority of reliefs, which depict events in the Buddha's life to the First Sermon, as described in the *Lalitavistara*, as well as episodes from *Jataka* stories about his previous lives. However, most reliefs on this section show scenes from the story of Sudhara, a young man following the Buddha's path to enlightenment related in the Mahayana *Gandhavyuha Sutra*, perhaps indicating that the whole monument itself is a massive "handbook" for the ordinary devotee.

The upper section of the monument has three circular terraces upon which stand the 72 hollow stupas, each containing a seated Buddha image. This section has been described as the world of formlessness, the stage at which the devotee attains awakening or Buddhahood: understanding the empty nature of all phenomena. This culmination is represented by a single empty stupa at the center or "peak" of the monument—symbolizing *nirvana*, the "snuffing out" of existence and end of rebirth in *samsara* with its attendant suffering. There are no reliefs on the three circular terraces, whose form suggests instead the tranquillity of infinity, without beginning or end.

Borobudur was probably abandoned a century or so after its creation, when the center of the Javanese kingdom shifted to the east of the island. Over the following centuries it gradually came to be covered in undergrowth and volcanic ash until nothing of the structure was visible. It was finally rediscovered by European investigators in the early nineteenth century, since when it has been extensively examined, reassembled (at least twice), and restored.

chapter 4

EAST ASIA

THE MAHAYANA TRADITION

CHINA

THE WAY OF THE BUDDHA

It is generally accepted that Buddhism arrived in China during the Han dynasty (206BCE– 220CE), when the earliest Buddhist communities grew up at the end of the desert Silk Road that brought Buddhist missionaries from India and Central Asia to China's northwest. Monks carrying texts and icons were among the mixed Chinese, Indian, and Central Asian populations who settled around the oasis of Dunhuang. For more than seven centuries, Dunhuang was a major center for the assimilation of Buddhist ideas, scriptures, and devotional art (see pages 114–117).

With its sensitivity to suffering and promise of salvation in a future existence, Buddhism took root in the disorder that followed the collapse of Han rule, and became further embedded in Chinese institutions under the Northern Wei emperors (386–534CE). The Northern Wei strongly encouraged Buddhism, and it was around this time, in the late fourth century, that the great cave temples at Yungang and Longmen, with their colossal Buddhist statuary, were first constructed (see pages 132–135). In this period the first wholly Chinese style of Buddhist image emerged, characterized by slim waists and delicate-featured, rounded faces. Earlier Chinese representations of the Buddha

had tended to depict him in non-Chinese clothes, and surviving fourth-century bronzes resemble the Indian Gandhara style (see Chapter Two), with the addition of a Chinese-style fiery *mandorla* (almond-shaped halo).

However, Buddhism remained a foreign religion, and a period of persecution in the mid-fifth century was just one of many obstacles to the spread of the Dharma. China was vast, the missionaries were few, and the Chinese had both social and philosophical reasons to repudiate the imported religion. The Buddhist ethics of monastic celibacy and universal salvationalism were incompatible with the Confucian emphasis on family and filial obedience. The Buddhist concept of rebirth in *samsara* (see page 26) was similarly alien to Confucians, whose ancestors bestowed their blessing on the living generations. Daoists who sought immortality through alchemical elixirs and other formulae were equally suspicious of the paradoxical Buddhist ideas expressed by those earlier non-Mahayana schools, such as the Theravada, which sought personal extinction in *nirvana*, and by Mahayana teachers who variously promised extinction and salvation in a Buddhist heaven (see pages 118–119).

YEARS OF GROWTH

A century after the Han collapse, China was convulsed by an invasion of Hun tribes from which the imperial court escaped in 311CE, leading to a division of the empire which lasted until 589CE. In the course of these centuries, Buddhism in China's

LEFT

The *bodhisattva* Avalokiteshvara (Guanyin) robed in an elaborate costume and standing on a lotus flower. This late 5th-century polychrome limestone carving illustrates the tendency by artisans of the Wei dynasty to give Buddhist figures an increasingly Chinese identity.

southern territories developed separately from the north, which was controlled by "barbarian" Hunnish or Turkic chieftains. Religion in the south in the fourth and fifth centuries was marked by the convergence of Daoist contemplative ideas and those of the Buddhist *prajña* (wisdom) school, whose respective speculations on the "nothingness" behind phenomena (Daoist *wu*) and "emptiness" (Buddhist *shunyata*) belonged, according to one thinker of the period, "to the same current." The southern Sangha also gained status and some autonomy during this period through its refusal to pay obeisance to secular rulers, and in this they found support from a new aristocracy which contributed to the endowment of Buddhist monasteries.

In the north, Buddhist teachers survived by allying themselves to the "barbarian" administrations, advising them in statecraft, and even by mesmerizing their civil and military leaders with displays of *siddhi* (magical power). But during the last decades of disunity the northern and southern Sanghas were increasingly in contact as newly translated texts in the north were taken south, and the northern "barbarian" rulers became increasingly Sinicized. By the outset of the unifying Sui dynasty (581–618CE), Buddhism was sufficiently integrated into all levels of Chinese society to serve, in itself, as a force in the unifying process. Under the shortlived Sui, a more naturalistic Buddhist representa-

tional style emerged that expressed greater anatomical awareness than was present in earlier Chinese sculpture, which had tended to favor more stiffly modeled figures.

Another stage in the process of acculturation lay in the translation and circulation of Buddhist texts. Two individuals of genius stand out. The first was Kumarajiva (344–413CE), a Central Asian monk who was summoned from the Silk Road oasis of Kucha to the northern capital of Chang'an (modern Xi'an). There, in the early fifth century, he directed an enormous team of scholars in the translation of Sanskrit texts. Through Kumarajiva, the Madhyamika ("Middle Path") treatises of the great second-century Indian scholar Nagarjuna (see page 55) and much of the *Prajñaparamita* (Perfection of Wisdom) literature entered the Chinese canon, with long-term consequences for the domestication of Mahayana ideas.

The other great scholar was Xuanzang (602–664CE) who went on a sixteen-year pilgrimage to India to collect Buddhist texts, returning to China in 645. The content of these so impressed the Tang emperor Taizong that he declared: "Looking at these works is like gazing at the sky or sea. They are so lofty one cannot measure their heights, so profound one cannot plumb their depths!" The Big Wild Goose pagoda in Xi'an was completed to house the many scriptures amassed by Xuanzang. The following emperor had less time for Buddhism, but his consort Wu Zetian, who outlived him and ruled alone as empress (690–705CE) in her own right, espoused Buddhism energetically, bringing it to the heart of palace life and instituting shrines and temples in many parts of the empire—as spectacularly exemplified at the Longmen caves.

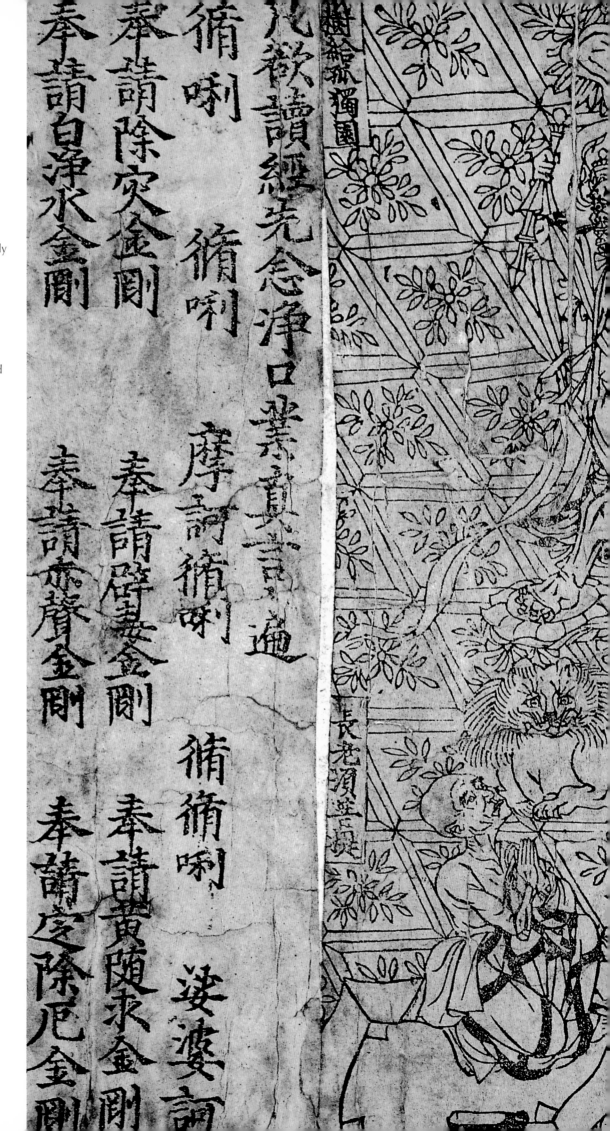

SHRINES OF THE OASIS

Muted tones mark this 10th-century painting on paper from Dunhuang of Guanyin by a lotus pond with a moon-like halo.

Dunhuang was one of the great centers of ancient Buddhist art and learning, but this tiny oasis town in the Gobi desert, hundreds of miles from the Chinese capital of Chang'an, was originally established by the Han emperor in the first century BCE as an army outpost in the struggle with invading Huns. The extent of military operations at this extreme western end of the Great Wall was revealed by Chinese archaeologists when, in excavations of 1944 and 1979, dozens of watch towers were uncovered along with military and administrative documents.

Once the Silk Road between India and western China had been secured from the north, Dunhuang grew rapidly. It became a vital Chinese entrepot for east- and west-bound traders, while, from the late third century CE, proselytizing Buddhist monks from India and Central Asia settled here to learn Chinese and to translate the Buddhist texts they had carried with them. This mingling of populations led to a rich cosmopolitan Buddhist culture and the creation of the magnificent cave shrines in an arid cliff-face at Mogao, about fifteen miles (25km) from Dunhuang.

THE CAVES OF THE THOUSAND BUDDHAS

The caves at Mogao, later known from their countless images as the Caves of the Thousand Buddhas, transformed the Dunhuang region into an important pilgrimage center until well into the fourteenth century. However, the high point of Buddhist

culture at Dunhuang came during the Tang dynasty (618–906CE). By then, almost five hundred caves, containing 45,000 square meters of wall painting and almost three thousand painted figurines, had been consecrated. This earliest Buddhist Chinese community had also generated a style of art which, like the ideas and texts that arrived at Dunhuang, was destined, for a limited time, to travel east to inform the cave sanctuaries at Yungang and Longmen (see pages 132–135).

After more than six centuries of neglect, the Mogao caves came to scholarly attention in the early twentieth century when a Daoist priest, Wang Yuanlu, rediscovered the shrines. The explorer Sir Aurel Stein, who arrived in 1907, persuaded Wang, in return for financial support for the restoration of the caves, to let him remove substantial collections of scrolls and paintings. Many of these were deposited in the British Museum. Stein's most spectacular trove came from Cave 17. This "library cave," as Stein called it, had been filled with thousands of manuscripts and hundreds of paint-

ings and then permanently sealed—either as protection from invaders or because the contents were no longer in use. Three years after Stein, the French Chinese scholar Paul Pelliot bought a second and even greater collection that was transported to the Musée Guimet and the Bibliothèque Nationale in Paris.

Four main genres were represented in the Dunhuang caves: paintings drawn directly onto the stuccoed shrine walls; paintings on silk and paper; three-dimensional stucco figures; and, not least, embroidery. Much of this embroidered silk consisted of decorated banners for use in colorful Mahayana rituals. The painting and sculpture, mainly depicting teaching Buddhas, Amitabha Buddha in his paradise, and protective *bodhisattvas*, were devotional. They were donated by laity whose portraits were often molded in stucco or added to the margins of a painted composition.

In the earlier centuries, artists from Buddhist India and Central Asia dominated the Dunhuang style, bringing with them a recognizably western idiom. The gorgeous red and black tones are reminiscent of Ajanta (see page 53). The form of the Buddha, in Indian robes and seated in lotus posture, likewise comes from the Indian Mahayana tradition. However, by the Tang period, the native Chinese love of line had penetrated the idiom, thus creating a unique style which combined elements of both eastern and western traditions.

PATHS TO SALVATION

CHINESE SCHOOLS AND MASTERS

Buddhism could only function as a unifying force within the Chinese state if the Sangha was kept under imperial control. With this in view, the Sui emperor appointed an abbot to take responsibility for the discipline of the entire Buddhist community. Periodic unrest was fomented by Mahayana demagogues on the basis of the theory that their era represented a final period of Buddhism before it became extinct, and by worshippers of the future Buddha, Maitreya, who proclaimed imminent world destruction. The Sui and Tang authorities, in collaboration with the Buddhist Sangha, were at pains to subdue these movements. Buddhism also amalgamated with existing Chinese folk religions, whose rituals and shrines dedicated to local deities received the added dimension of a Buddhist identity, and this gave it vigorous and colorful popular life.

While major Buddhist texts had been imported from India, their translation into Chinese was just one aspect of domestication. A number of charismatic teachers in the sixth and seventh centuries founded schools that assumed an increasingly Chinese character.

PURE LAND AND CHAN

Pure Land doctrine, which reached China during the unsettled period that followed the collapse of the Han dynasty, developed from an Indian Mahayana theory of the first and second centuries CE. The cult of Amitabha, the Buddha of Infinite Radiance, evolved into a salvationist path offering rebirth in a "Pure Land" which was presided over by celestial Buddhas and compassionate *bodhisattvas*, and where those who suffered in this life could enjoy a happy rebirth without having achieved enlightenment on earth. The most desirable of these heavens was

LEFT

A 6th-century limestone relief
carving of the late Northern Wei
dynasty (386–534CE) showing
a smiling Buddha backed by a
nimbus of lotus petals. His face
and neck bear traces of gilding.
Six joyful celestial figures adorn
the upper register of the almond-
shaped *mandorla*. The figure was
among a hoard of fine, mostly
6th-century statues found in 1996
in the grounds of a long-vanished
Buddhist temple in Qingzhou,
Shandong province. They had
been carefully buried in the
12th century, perhaps because
they were old and beyond repair
(most are damaged), or because
of religious persecution.

OPPOSITE

A stone Buddhist votive stele
dedicated by a family named
Yan and dated 557CE, during the
Northern Qi dynasty (550–577CE).
The main register shows the
Buddha enthroned, flanked by
bodhisattvas, all with *mandorla*s.

LEFT
A painted limestone Buddha from
the Qingzhou cache. The figure
shows the more rounded, sensual
style of the Northern Qi dynasty
(550–577CE), compared with the
restrained grace of Northern Wei
sculptures, found in the same
cache and dating from only a few
decades earlier (see page 119).

Sukhavati, the Paradise of the West, which was the realm of Amitabha Buddha (in Chinese, Amituo Fo) and his manifestation Avalokiteshvara, the *bodhisattva* of compassion. A Mahayana Sanskrit *sutra* called the *Sukhavativyuha* describes this paradise as a place of happiness and beauty where all without exception can hear the Buddha preaching.

By the time the cult of Amitabha had arrived in China, this new and popular Mahayana sect taught that to enter Sukhavati, it was necessary merely to focus the mind on Amitabha for seven nights or to recite the mantra *Nianfo Amituo Fo* ("Homage to Amitabha Buddha"). The cult was particularly successful in southern China following a translation of the *Sukhavativyuha* by Ji Qian, a monk from Central Asia who worked under the protection of the southern emperor in the first decades of the third century. The cult of Avalokiteshvara (Guanyin) was integrally related to Pure Land devotion, and many Guanyin figures show the *bodhisattva* carrying the emblem of Amitabha prominently in her headdress.

Chan, the school of meditation, represented another development of the Mahayana which would would have far-reaching influence on the development of Buddhism—particularly in Korea and Japan where it continues to thrive as Son and Zen respectively. Chan, from the Sanskrit *dhyana* (meditation) is reputed to have

originated with the teachings of an Indian monk named Bodhidharma who traveled to China in the early sixth century. Although Bodhidharma is said to have brought with him the long and complex *Lankavatara-sutra* from which much of Chan doctrine derives, this Chinese school of "meditation only" repudiated both text-based Buddhism and ritual devotions, emphasizing the existence within every being of a "Buddha nature" which could be realized in silent, introspective meditation. "Direct pointing" to the Dharma thereby became a natural process, akin to the iconoclastic principles of Chinese Daoist sages who retreated from society and the world of action to cultivate lives of intelligent idleness and contemplation.

A convergence, in southern China during the period of disunity, of unadorned Buddhist meditation and the intellectual freedom of Daoism evolved into a culture that necessarily produced teachers and monastic centers. Chan masters nonetheless continued to transmit their teachings orally, and the paradoxical wisdom and witty conversations of Chan patriarchs are recorded in a number of anthologies which later formed the basis of Korean Son and Japanese Zen practice.

In addition to the masters who established the schools of Pure Land and Chan, one prominent figure was the scholar Zhiyi (538–598CE) who digested and systematized the entirety of the Buddhist canon and at Mount Tiantai (Zhejiang province) established a school based on his interpretation of the *Lotus Sutra* (*Saddharmapundarika-sutra*). This declared that the historical Buddha was an earthly avatar of an eternal Buddha, and that all canonical texts had their place at different stages of the Buddha's teaching, which each devotee could reach according to their level of understanding. Just as, according to Zhiyi in a celebrated dictum, "every speck of dust and every

ABOVE
The 10th-century dynasty stone pagoda at Kaiyuan temple in Quangzhou, Fujian province. Combining the stupa with the traditional Chinese gate-tower, and perhaps also inspired by multiroofed Nepalese forms, the pagoda is a distinctive Chinese contribution to East Asian Buddhist architecture. From the 10th to 12th centuries an octagonal plan predominated; pagodas became less common thereafter owing to the rise of Chan (Zen), which did not include worship in or around pagodas as part of its rituals.

moment of thought contained the universe," so the *Lotus Sutra* represented a summation of the entire Dharma, even though it was only one text in the canon. Tiantai, as this school came to be known, held that simply to recite the Lotus represented a path to salvation. The *Lotus Sutra* became the most popular and influential sutra in East Asian Buddhism (see also pages 168–169).

Another significant Chinese sect of the Mahayana was Huayan, whose leading interpreter, Fazang (643–712CE), had been an assistant in Xuanzang's office of translation. In 704CE, Empress Wu summoned Fazang to explain the *Flower Garland Sutra* (Sanskrit *Avatamsaka-sutra*, Chinese *Huayan Jing*, hence the name of the school). The outcome of this meeting was Fazang's influential *Essay on the Golden Lion*, which expounded the Huayan analysis of the emptiness (*shunyata*) doctrine. In this, Fazang explained that *shunyata* manifested on two levels: the quintessential (*li*) and the dynamic or manifest (*shih*). The gold of a sculpted golden lion, to which he pointed during his interview with the empress, was a symbol of *li*, while the lion's form was *shih*. Just as gold pervaded every part of the statue, so all phenomena are manifestations of a single essence (*li*) which is empty of an identity that can be differentiated.

Fazang also explained this concept to his followers by surrounding a lamp with eight mirrors and demonstrating how one phenomenon (the lamp—an early Buddhist symbol for the Dharma) could be infinitely reflected within its participating environment without any sacrifice of essence.

Carved into a cliff-face at the confluence of three great rivers at Leshan in Sichuan province is the giant figure of Maitreya (Mile), the Buddha of the future age. Begun in 713CE and completed in 803CE, the world's largest stone Buddha rises 234 feet (71m) from its feet at near water level to its head at the clifftop. According to Mahayana tradition, the world will experience a "dark age" of disorder in which the Dharma will decay, to be restored in a future epoch by the coming of the next Buddha, Maitreya. Periods of unrest in imperial China sometimes spawned messianic movements centered on Maitreya, whose followers believed the new age was imminent.

THE GLORIES OF THE TANG

In 618CE the young emperor Gaozu (618–626CE) established the Tang dynasty (618–907CE), which brought unity to the empire, at least for the first two centuries of the dynasty. These centuries brought an enormous expansion in trade with the West, unprecedented national prosperity, and a great flowering of the visual arts, music, and poetry. The Tang capital at Chang'an (Xi'an) became a vast and elegantly laid out cosmopolitan city containing both Chinese and visiting populations from the North and from as far as the Middle East. Within a milieu of religious tolerance for nonindigenous faiths, Buddhism—despite periods of persecution in the mid-ninth century—received imperial support from rulers such as Taizong and the empress Wu (see pages 111 and 122). Countless monasteries and temples were established during the period. None have survived intact, but seventh-century Japanese buildings of Tang design may be seen at the Horyuji temple complex in Nara.

Buddhism during the Tang penetrated Chinese daily life as never before. In 838CE the Japanese monk Ennin visited the mountains of Mount Wutai, sacred to the *bodhisattva* Manjushri, where more than three hundred temples were built during the Tang. There, on the road and in towns and villages, he witnessed the fervor of monks, pilgrims, and common people—a phenomenon that proved relatively shortlived in China but was to have far-reaching consequences for the development of Buddhism in Japan. This was the heyday of Chinese Buddhism, and the Buddhist virtue of generosity (*shila*) filtered down from the imperial court and wealthy monasteries as shrines, hospitals, and public works were funded by the state and, not infrequently, administered by the Sangha.

Many of the great Tang poets were deeply influenced by Buddhism and evoked both its institutional and contemplative aspects. At one extreme, in an early ninth-century poem, Bo Juyi (772–846CE) described the jade and gold decoration of a monastic image hall, where "white Buddhas sit like ranks of trees." At the other extreme, the meditative life is evoked by poets such as Hanshan, who described the poverty and solitude of the hermit life while still holding fast to his contemplative "pearl of the mind."

ABOVE
Two horsemen in a landscape, identified as Siddhartha, the Buddha-to-be, and his equerry Chandaka. This beautifully drawn fragment of a 7th-century painting on stone is one of the tiny number of Tang paintings to survive to the present day.

A silver gilt storage container for compacted bricks of tea. The container, which is decorated with bird designs, was discovered in an underground chamber at the pagoda of Famen temple in 1987 together with a set of reliquary caskets (see previous pages). Located not far from the Tang capital of Chang'an, Famen was a wealthy monastery that enjoyed the patronage of several Tang emperors.

The great artistic achievements of the Tang were not on a monumental scale, although in late examples of stone carving at Longmen and in cave-temples at Mount Tianlong in Shanxi province, Tang artists imprinted rare expressions of humane Buddhism in what, by now, they had fashioned into an indigenous style. At Longmen (see pages 132–135), one *bodhisattva* stands with an expression of serenity and compassion, right hand elegantly raised in the "fear-allaying gesture" (*abhayamudra*). In clinging robes decorated with exquisitely carved strings of jewels, this smiling, sublime savior with its rounded face and limbs, is unmistakably Chinese. At Tianlong, Buddhas and *bodhisattvas*, depicted in scarcely arrested movement, become yet more humanized: regal, but no longer dependent on the Indian princely ideal which formerly had been the prototype of earlier *bodhisattva* imagery.

Another aspect of this process of domestication lay in the translation of China's popular *bodhisattva* Avalokiteshvara into the protective female deity Guanyin. Just before the Tang accession, Sui artists had brought naturalistic representation of the human form to a perfection which combined exquisite human beauty with an ethereal spirituality. By contrast, Guanyin figures of the Tang (see page 123) have a warm and comforting presence, which by the mid-ninth century had become courtly and sensual. This emphasis on the living form, most often depicted in three-dimensional ceramic figures, was characteristic of the Tang, although towards the end of the dynasty the genre became over-eroticized and decadent.

Up until the Tang the "Chinese" face had been entirely stylized by artists, and both gesture and costume had been rendered according to convention. One aesthetic development during the Tang lay in the creation of portrait images. This tendency was reflected in the later shrines constructed at Dunhuang (see pages 114–117), in which a Buddha figure in stucco would be placed among portrait figurines of the shrine's donors—one intensely lifelike Dunhuang Buddha itself vividly suggests the presence of a living sage.

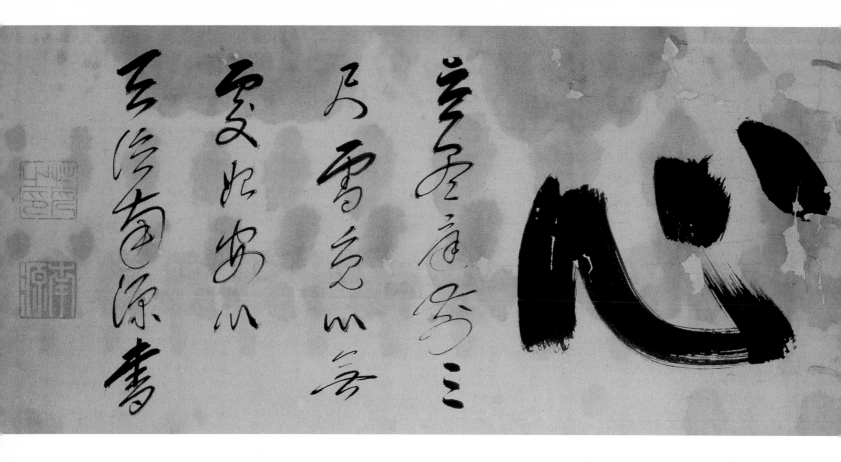

ABOVE
Calligraphy by the 17th-century
Chinese Buddhist monk Nangen,
from the Mampukuji monastery
near Kyoto, Japan. Founded in
1661 by Chinese Chan monks,
the monastery was a major
conduit for Chinese culture
to Tokugawa Japan. The large
central character is the word
for "heart."

OPPOSITE
Cloisonné mandalas in the form
of a building with a pagoda-style
finial, were popular in the reign
of the Qing emperor Qianlong
(1736–95); this one bears the date
1772. *Cloisonné*, a technique
learned from Byzantium, involved
applying glass paste to metal.

By contrast, painted silks from Dunhuang's Tang period present a variety of genres. On the one hand, portrait images of donors are given their place at the margins of the main devotional registers. On the other, many of these silk hangings continue to depict conventionalized *bodhisattvas*, whose features, dress, and color remain in Indian and Central Asian style.

Almost every aspect of the visual arts were represented in Tang imperial tombs, where *ming qi*, or "articles of the spirit," were buried. These included Buddhist guardian figures alongside ceramic vessels, figurines of royal attendants, and the famous and splendidly lifelike Tang camels and horses in colorfully glazed porcelain.

The astonishing fluidity of Tang draughtsmanship may be surmised both from tomb paintings and from Japanese copies of the work of Tang painters who traveled to Japan. A catalogue of the twelfth-century imperial collection lists several hundred Tang paintings, many on Buddhist subjects. However, apart from these works, almost all Tang Buddhist art had been destroyed during religious persecutions in 845CE, when tens of thousands of Buddhist temples and shrines were obliterated.

The glorious history of Tang painting is haunted by the name of a great artist whose work is known only by repute and imitation. Wu Dao Zi was renowned during his lifetime as the greatest figure painter of the period. Court patronage sent Wu to adorn the walls of important Buddhist monasteries and temples, both in Chang'an and the provinces. But none of his works, beyond copies and legendary accounts of his prolific genius, has survived.

Nevertheless, the Buddhist forms that emerged during the Tang were largely maintained under the Song dynasty (960–1279). A major new development in Chinese Buddhist art began with the arrival of the Yuan (Mongol) dynasty (1279–1368), who established Beijing as China's capital. The Mongols followed the Tibetan form of Buddhism, and a distinctive Sino-Tibetan style of art and architecture evolved alongside traditional Chinese forms. One early example is the White Pagoda, which forms part of Beijing's Miaoying monastery. Despite its name, this is not a traditional Chinese pagoda but a stupa in the Tibetan style.

This style was further developed under China's last dynasty, the Qing, or Manchu (1644–1912), who also followed Tibetan Buddhism. They marked the advent of their dynasty by erecting a stupa similar to the White Stupa in Beijing's Beihai Park. Chinese planning allied to Tibetan architectural styles can also be seen at temples such as Puning in Chengde (Jehol), Hebei province, constructed by the Qing emperor Qianlong (1736–1795).

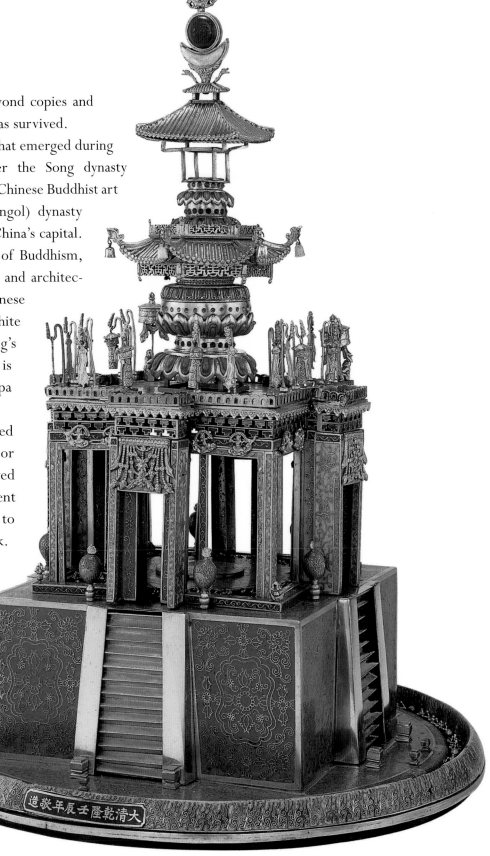

CAVES OF THE RADIANT BUDDHA

BELOW

The face of a giant Buddha figure on the north wall of Cave 20 at Yungang, attended by a standing bodhisattva. The 5th-century image was dedicated by a ruler of the Northern Wei dynasty. The imposing, squared face may derive from the styles of the Gandharan regions; the pupils of the eyes were drilled at a later period.

The construction of the Yungang cave shrines in northern Shanxi province came at a complicated but significant moment in Chinese Buddhist history. Between 444 and 542CE, the emperor Taiwu—a Turkic ruler of the Northern Wei dynasty—had conducted a violent campaign against Buddhism, and his grandson and successor Wencheng was anxious to create new monuments to compensate for the temples and icons obliterated during the previous dispensation. The site of Yungang, an exposed cliff-face that runs for more than half a mile (1km) along the Wuzhou River, was chosen for its easily worked sandstone and its proximity to the imperial city of Pingcheng (today's Datong). Here, for thirty years from ca. 460CE, tens of thousands of masons, supervised initially by the charismatic monk Tanyao, worked to excavate some fifty grottoes, from whose walls they would fashion over fifty thousand statues and intricately carved and painted niches.

Many of the artisans who were drafted to work at Yungang came directly from Dunhuang where they had created painting and stucco sculpture in idioms transposed from India and Central Asia (see Chapter Two). At Yungang they adapted their skills to carving solid rock, and the scale of the site, with its multistory shrines and five colossal Buddhas, represented an enormous gesture of zeal which still radiates from the worn sandstone. The most celebrated of the monumental figures at Yungang is the meditating Buddha in Cave 20, whose massive torso and square-cut features are balanced by the spiritual tranquility expressed by the figure's half-smile. This masterwork of early Chinese Buddhist carving retains some elements of monumental Indian prototypes. In the later Yungang caves, this heroic western aesthetic converges with a more fluid Chinese style. The crowds of *bodhisattvas*, heavenly spirits, and devotees who surround

the Buddha in Cave 6 are slender and mobile, and their features increasingly Chinese, a tendency that would be developed at the Longmen caves in the late fifth century.

CELESTIAL VISIONS: LONGMEN

When the imperial court moved south to Luoyang in Henan province in 494, Buddhism was entrenched further as the Wei dynasty's religion by the creation of cave shrines at Longmen, about ten miles (16km) from the capital. In contrast to the fragile rock at Yungang, the hard grey limestone of Longmen offered Wei artists the scope for both bold, monumental statements of their faith and a more delicate approach which introduced into stone carving line-drawing styles from south China.

There are twelve main caves at Longmen, most of them designed more symmetrically than those at Yungang, some also reflecting new developments in Mahayana, such as Pure Land and Tantra. Among Longmen's most celebrated images is the great Amitabha Buddha, flanked by the Buddha's disciples Ananda and Mahakashyapa in the Binyang cave (ca. 520CE). Backed by the soaring flames of a *mandorla* and a halo of petals, this Buddha of Infinite Radiance sits vividly awake, his hands, both beautifully preserved, in the "fear-allaying" and "boon-bestowing" gestures. A later figure of Vairochana, a cosmic Buddha of the Tantric pantheon, was commissioned during the early Tang (672CE); nearby stand two fierce figures, probably Dharmapalas or "protectors of the Dharma". In contrast are relief carvings of courtiers executed in suave, almost calligraphic lines, as though "brushed" into stone as they pay homage to the hieratic and enlightened principals.

ABOVE
These ferocious figures on the north wall of the Longmen grottoes have been identified as Buddhist guardians. A heavenly king holds aloft a Buddhist stupa, alongside the heroic protective warrior Vajrapani ("Thunderbolt–Carrier") who in the Indian Mahayana represented the power of the Buddha. The notion of spiritual guardianship came originally from Hindu tradition.

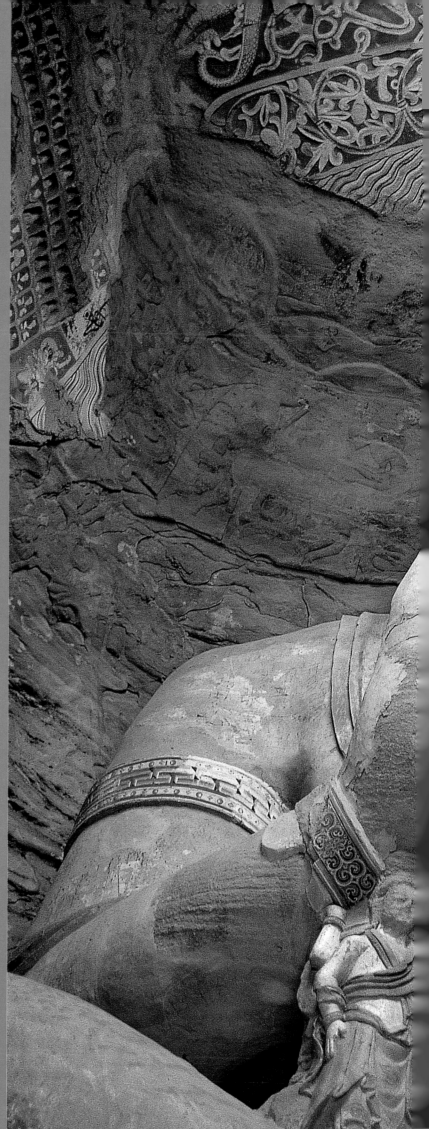

ABOVE

A polychrome relief from Yungang showing various Buddhist figures, including Maitreya (top, with crossed legs) and the Buddha (below right). The Yungang reliefs incorporate architectural details that give an idea of the original elaborate wooden facades that once formed the cave entrances.

RIGHT

The colossal 5th-century Buddha Maitreya in Cave 13 of Yungang is one of the most imposing of the monumental figures in the complex. A convergence of Indian, Central Asian, and a more emphatically national style can be seen in the modeling of this image. But the influence of Dunhuang artists who were brought to work at Yungang is especially strong in the decoration of the shrine walls.

KOREA

THE HARMONY OF ORDER

BELOW

An unglazed earthenware tile with a dragon or monster design. Such tiles were placed on the roofs of Korean Buddhist temples and other important buildings to protect them from harmful spirits, an idea that originated in China. Unified Silla dynasty, 7th–9th century CE.

Buddhism first came to Korea in 372CE, when the missionary monk Shundao (Korean, Sundo) arrived from China with texts and Buddha images and introduced the Mahayana Dharma to northern Korean and Manchurian populations. The conquest of Korea by the Han in 108BCE led to four hundred years of a Chinese presence on the peninsula. When the Han colonists were forced out in the fourth century CE, the country divided into three independent kingdoms: Koguryo in north, Paekche in the west, and Silla in the southeast, until the Silla overran and unified the entire peninsula in the seventh century.

Most aspects of pre-Buddhist Korean culture have been obliterated by internal wars and invasions. But something of the vigor of the early indigenous peoples may be sensed from northern Koguryo tombs, whose walls and ceilings are covered with the earliest surviving Korean paintings—most famously vivid scenes depicting archers on horseback and hunted animals. These dazzling painted compositions sometimes include Buddhist iconographic elements such as scrolls and lotuses which, along with some small clay Buddhas, suggest a rudimentary synthesis of Buddhist and pre-Buddhist funerary ritual.

ASSIMILATION AND GROWTH

This blending of Buddhism with local nature religions would characterize the Korean Dharma from the outset. Buddhism took on a national character in Korea by accommodating itself with shamanist cults and even integrating aspects of these cults into monastic ritual. The famous *seungmu* dance, which is performed by

BELOW
An incense burner for use in
Buddhist temple ritual, with the
Sanskrit mantra *Om ram svaha*
within a decorative circle. Bronze
inlaid with silver, Koryo period,
918–1392CE.

monks in robes with long fluttering sleeves to the rhythmic beat of drums, had its origin in shamanist ritual, while the many Buddhist temples built on Korean mountaintops have always maintained shrines to mountain spirits. When Buddhism became the state-protected religion of the Silla, a Mahayana legend that dragons or serpent deities (*nagas*) had guarded the Buddha's esoteric doctrine in the underworld until the Indian Sangha was ready to comprehend it, became fused in Korea with indigenous snake and dragon cults. One Silla monarch who died in 681CE vowed to be reborn as a dragon which would protect both state and religion.

While the Koguryo people were the first in Korea to adopt Buddhism, missionary monks arrived at Paekche in 384CE, leading to the establishment of the Madhyamika (Middle Way) and Tiantai sects, and by the sixth century Buddhism had become the state religion in the Paekche kingdom. It was from Paekche, with its vigorous seafaring culture, that Buddhist missionaries and traders reached Japan. Two Avalokiteshvara figures at the Horyuji temple at Nara are thought to be based on images from Paekche and were perhaps even created by Korean artists.

On account of its distance from Chinese influence, Silla was the last of the Korean kingdoms to adopt Buddhism, which it did in 582CE. But by the time the country had been unified under the Silla in 668CE, five major Mahayana schools—among them the Vinaya

school of monastic discipline, Huayan (see page 122), Yogachara ("Consciousness Only"), and a new Korean syncretic school—were established on the peninsula. By the seventh century CE, Buddhist thought in Korea had developed to the extent that influential Korean monks were contributing to the development of Mahayana in the Chinese Buddhist "homeland."

One aspect of Silla military and religious dominance that continues to fascinate today was the role of a fighting force called the Hwarang ("Flowering Manhood"). Created in 576CE, this ascetic military elite, which spearheaded the conquest of Koguryo and Paekche, is thought to have originated some of the martial arts practiced today. Inspired by a combination of Confucian, Daoist, and Buddhist ideas, they were typically Korean in their religious syncretism. Like many Korean Mahayanists, they were also associated with the cult of the future Buddha Maitreya (Korean, Miruk), while their dances derived from shamanistic rituals.

The Silla also came to dominate the peninsula through an alliance with Tang armies, and it was partly through this association with China that the United Silla Period (668–935CE) became a time of high prosperity and artistic achievement. Buddhist philosophy flourished during the Silla era, leading to a benign and nonsectarian fusion of disparate Mahayana schools, in particular the Madhyamika ("Middle Way") and the

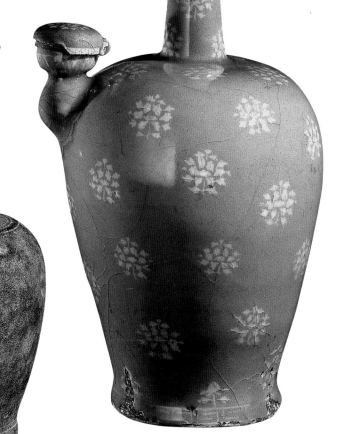

Yogachara ("Mind Only"). The Silla capital, Kyongju, became one of the world's richest cities: Pulguksa temple, with its two celebrated pagodas (see pages 144–145) attests to the majesty of other Buddhist temples built here during the period.

Of equal national and long-term historical importance is the eighth-century Haeinsa temple, which was also built during the United Silla Period. Since the early fifteenth century, Haeinsa temple has been the home of one of Korea's outstanding national treasures. This is the *Tripitaka Koreana*, the entire canon of Buddhist *sutra*s, *vinaya*, and *abhidharma* (discourses, works on monastic discipline, and commentaries) inscribed in more than fifty-two million exquisitely carved Chinese characters. Existing as eighty thousand finely carved woodblocks and housed today in two special depositories at Haeinsa temple, this version of the *Tripitaka*, which became the basis of the later Japanese rescension, has a long and dramatic history. In addition to their formidable land and sea forces, the dynastic leaders of medieval Korea would, in times of national crisis, turn to the protective power of the Buddha, and when the Koryo state faced invasion from Mongolia in the early thirteenth century, this new and complete version of the Tripitaka was created as a protective talisman for national defense.

The main hall, dating from 1818, of the Haeinsa temple complex, west of Taegu in present-day South Korea, originally built in the early 9th century. Wood and iron statues of Vairochana Buddha and five *bodhisattvas* surmount the elaborately decorated altar.

OPPOSITE

A crowned *bodhisattva* in gilded wood, from the 15th century during the Choson dynasty (1392–1910). The hands are represented in the *vitarka mudra*, or gesture of teaching.

From 1236 to 1251, more than eighty thousand birchwood blocks were carved, and while the original monastery buildings which housed them no longer exist, the Tripitaka has survived completely intact. It is said that the birch wood on which the blocks were carved was seasoned by boiling it for three years in sea water, followed by a prolonged drying process. Many Korean temples are dedicated to one of the "Three Gems" of Buddhism—the Buddha, the Dharma (teaching), and the Sangha (community of monks). Haeinsa temple became associated with the Dharma when the *Tripitaka* was deposited within its precincts. These woodblocks are probably the oldest anywhere in existence that can still be used for printing.

SON AND THE RISE OF KORYO

Son Buddhism (Chinese Chan, Japanese Zen) entered Korea during the Silla period and rapidly established itself. Attracted by the reputation of Chan teachers who had repudiated textual learning in favor of meditation, Korean monks dissatisfied with their own training in scholastic Buddhism traveled to China to study with Chan masters, notably with the fourth Chan patriarch, Daoxin (580–651CE). The monks who

brought Daoxin's practice to Korea eventually established the Mount Huiyang school (879CE), which was the first of the "Nine Mountain Schools" of Son. These have dominated Korean Buddhism from the ninth century to the present era.

The Silla kingdom declined during the same years as the dissolution of the Tang in China, and the early history of the succeeding Koryo dynasty (918–1392) was compromised by invading Mongols under Kublai Khan, who colonized the peninsula in 1258. While Korean cultural identity became partially submerged by Mongol rule, Buddhism and the Buddhist arts of metal-casting and temple architecture continued to thrive under the sponsorship of the state.

While Son remained the dominant sect, learned or scholastic Buddhism continued to hold sway in the urban centers. Two Son masters who attempted to reconcile the scholastic and meditational paths stand out during the Koryo dynasty. Uich'on (1055–1101), like many of his predecessors, traveled to China, where he studied Chan among a number of other Buddhist disciplines. Returning to Korea with the intention of healing the rift between Son and textually-based Buddhism, Uich'on's teaching emphasized the "parallel cultivation of doctrinal study and meditation." Uich'on died before he could complete his work, but his teaching was taken in a new direction by Chinul (1158–1210), who founded the Chogye school of Son, subtly adapting Chan "sudden enlightenment" doctrine to the application of textual study, whose goal was the gradual acquisition of wisdom (Sanskrit *prajña*). Chinul's synthesis of these paths became the practical basis the Chogye school of Son.

Toward the end of the Koryo dynasty, Buddhism lost its central place in Korean religious and philosophical life. By the beginning of the Choson dynasty, in 1392, a new Confucian orthodoxy withdrew support for the Sangha and Korean Buddhism suffered a decline. But the practice of intuitive meditation in remote mountain temples, which depended neither on state support nor textual learning, survived, and Son has continued as Korea's leading school of Buddhism to this day.

PULGUKSA AND SOKKURAM

TEMPLES OF THE TRIPLE GEM

Among the most significant Buddhist monuments in Korea is Pulguksa, or Bulguksa ("Temple of the Buddha Land"), which was established in the Unified Silla period. Like most Silla and Koryo temples, Pulguksa was built high in the mountains, which allowed it to escape the destruction that befell the majority of urban Buddhist buildings in the fourteenth century under the new Confucian dispensation of the Choson dynasty.

However, the temple was largely destroyed by the Mongols and then, in the sixteenth century, by the Japanese. The stone foundations, stairways, and pagodas remained from the original eighth-century structure, and these provided the basis for a remarkable restoration project completed in the late 1970s. The extant stone remains were restored, and vanished wooden buildings were reconstructed using ancient methods. Visitors today gain a vivid impression of the original splendor of the temple, which served as the main shrine for the Silla capital of Kyongju (Gyeongju), ten miles (16km) to the northwest, once one of East Asia's greatest cities.

As with the architecture of India, Korean temples were built according to sacred principles, the Korean design being in *mandala* form, with the temple hall at the center of the monastic precincts. The middle of a *mandala* represents the area of the greatest sacred value, therefore it is significant that Pulguksa once lay within a small lake which separated worldly space from the holy sphere of the temple.

Before the main hall stand two original stone pagodas now revered as among Korea's most valued national treasures. The Shakyamuni stupa, twenty-four feet (7m) in height, is built in relatively conventional Chinese style, and was believed to enshrine relics of the historical Buddha. The second stupa, the Prabhutaratna, stands over thirty

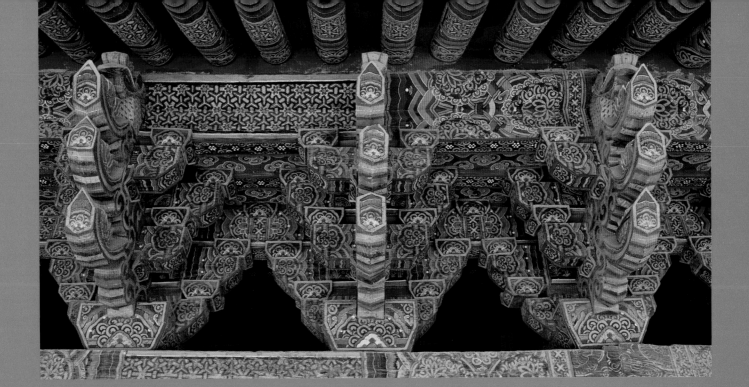

feet (9m) high and is unique in design, having four stair-ways leading to its lowest platform, and above this four tiers in differing patterns with an octagonal upper roof.

Above Pulguksa, a little farther up the wooded slopes of Mount Toham, is the pilgrimage site of Sokkuram (Seokguram) grotto, begun in the mid-eighth century and recalling the Buddhist tradition of cave temples. The small antechamber is dominated by guardian deities with raised fists, and reliefs of thirty other figures appear on the walls of the antechamber, vestibule, and circular main shrine, some of them in niches above the principal statue. The latter is a magnificent granite representation of the Buddha making the *bhumisparsha mudra*, touching the earth at the moment of his enlightenment.

TOP
A detail of the underside of the roof of Pulguksa temple, showing the multiple wooden brackets that support the heavy overhanging eaves, both features inspired by Chinese models. The brackets are decorated in a variety of symbolic colors in intricate patterns.

RIGHT
The great 8th-century granite Buddha in Sokkuram grotto. The massive body is adorned with a simple but naturalistically carved robe. The full face, with its small nose and a mouth still bearing traces of the original red paint, is typical of the Silla period.

JAPAN

REFINING THE PATH

 The cradle of Japanese civilization in the early sixth century CE lay in the Asuka Valley in the fertile plains of Yamato, where the first "Great Kings" held sway over the aristocratic clans of southwest Japan from their capital of Naniwa (today's Osaka). It was here, as an integral component in vigorous cultural contacts between Japan and the Korean state of Paekche, that Buddhism entered Japanese aristocratic culture. Initially, in 513CE, the Paekche monarch dispatched a Confucian scholar to Yamato. This gift from Paekche was followed in 552CE by a Buddhist missionary, an image of the Buddha (Butsu in Japanese), some Buddhist texts, craftsmen specializing in Buddhist iconography, and a letter proclaiming the "higher wisdom" and both the promise of salvation and the threat of karmic retribution.

THE PRINCE AND THE DHARMA

It was during the reign of the Empress Suiko (592–628CE) and her regent, Prince Shotoku, that Buddhism was most vigorously promoted. Shotoku, who was the first prominent Japanese Buddhist, used the Dharma as a part of a radical reorganization of Japanese court administration along Chinese lines. His famous "Seventeen Article Constitution" of 604CE proposed a state order dependent on the Confucian ideal of harmony between heaven, earth, and man, with the emperor as heaven's representative on earth. The first article in the Constitution enjoins Confucian harmony, the second orders that "the Three Buddhist Treasures [Buddha, Dharma, Sangha] should be sincerely reverenced … for these are supreme objects of faith."

The arrival of Buddhism also coincided with a rise of the powerful Soga clan, whose leaders had been instrumental in centralizing Yamato court government. Buddhism thus entered court life in part so as to inspire it with new spiritual and ethical authority. This found its place in the context of a

ABOVE
Small wooden stupas from the
Nara period, mid-8th century CE.
Empress Suiko commissioned a
million of these stupas to contain
thanksgiving prayers for victory
over a rebellion in 764CE. Many
were donated to monasteries in
the Kansai region. The prayers are
the earliest surviving examples of
printed Japanese.

OPPOSITE
This standing wooden *bodhisattva*
(*bosatsu*) of the Nara period (710–
794CE) is inspired by the sculpture
of Tang China. The full figure
and close fitting robe are Tang
features, as are the looped bands
of drapery. The gestures (*mudras*)
of the now handless figure cannot
be known precisely; one hand
was probably raised, perhaps
in *vitarka mudra* (teaching) or
abhaya mudra (fear-allaying),
and one lowered, perhaps in
varada mudra (gift-bestowing).

traditional Shinto religion whose flexible and contemplative aesthetic would prove sympathetic to both the dynamism and serenity of the Buddhist Dharma. However, the initial struggle between Buddhists and Shinto traditionalists led to periodic destruction, until the end of the seventh century, of the earliest Buddhist monuments. A brief civil war in 588CE had seen defeat for the traditionalists, and in the peace that followed, the charismatic Shotoku commissioned temple building and encouraged a devotional Buddhism based on the worship of the historical Buddha and divine beings such as the future Buddha, Maitreya (Japanese, Miroku), and the compassionate *bodhisattva* Avalokiteshvara (Japanese, Kannon or Kwannon). Shotoku's influence suffered at the hands of his own clan in the late seventh century, and the Wakakusadera, the temple he built next to his own residence outside Nara, was burned down in 670CE. But the new religion had taken hold among the Yamato aristocracy and they soon constructed the celebrated Horyuji monastery on the site of the Wakakusadera.

THE TEMPLE OF THE GOLDEN HALL

Chinese temples from early times had been modeled on palace architecture, and this model, transmitted via Korea, was now reproduced and modified by Korean architects and craftsmen at Horyuji near Nara. Oriented on a north-south axis, the Chinese temple consisted of tiled wooden buildings raised on terraces in a walled courtyard.

The Golden Hall of the Horyuji temple complex, Nara. Built to replace an earlier temple burnt in 670CE, Horyuji was inspired by Chinese models by way of Korea; it was largely designed and constructed by Korean hands. The hall (*kondo*) and the nearby five-storied pagoda are among the world's oldest wooden buildings.

Entering through a ceremonial gateway, the worshipper was led in a straight line to a main hall and to a pagoda which together dominated the compound. At Horyuji, worshippers entered at a gate to the south and then turned either to the east to approach the magnificent five-storied pagoda, or west to face the "Golden Hall." This modification of mainland layout established a prototype for almost all later Japanese temples and suggests an early beginning to the formalized asymmetry that characterized other genres of Japanese Buddhist art.

One surprising stylistic throwback at Horyuji lay in the styles of sculpture that adorned the temple buildings. These were from the hand of Shiba Tori and his assistants and include works in camphor wood, red pine (imported from Korea), and bronze. Some of these are in the austere, stiff, somewhat archaic but spiritually exalted manner achieved by Koguryo monks of the previous century in northern Korea (see page 136). Other pieces, such as a figure of Maitreya and a *bodhisattva* in the Chuguji convent at Horyuji, are similarly archaic in style, but rounder in form and softly expressive of profound states of meditation. These figures alone attest to the extraordinary impact on the Japanese mind that Buddhism had already achieved.

THE FLOWERING OF THE DHARMA

In 710CE the capital moved to Nara and the new imperial city, with its grid pattern of wide streets, temples, and palaces, was laid out along the lines of the Chinese capital of Chang'an (Xi'an). During the Nara period (710–794CE), Buddhism would become a national religion, and the Japanese aristocracy would increasingly adopt the cultural values of China. Just as Chang'an during this period became a cosmopolitan city, so Nara was filled with Chinese and Korean monks, scholars, and artists whose teaching, craftsmanship, and styles of dress were taken up by the Nara elite.

The institutionalization of Buddhism was a major component in this process of acculturation. As in Korea, Buddhism was adopted in the interest of protecting the welfare of the state. Hence,

a smallpox epidemic in 738CE prompted the emperor Shomu (701–756)—who later abdicated to become a Buddhist monk—to order the construction of the immense Todaiji temple complex. Priests and scholars had already brought six schools of the Mahayana from China to Japan, but the sect that found favor with the Nara court was Kegon (the Chinese Huayan; see page 122), which centered on the universal Buddha Vairochana (Japanese, Rushana). Todaiji's gargantuan Vairochana Buddha not only absorbed the energies of thousands of craftsmen but also used up all the copper in Japan, almost bankrupting the state it was designed to protect. The copper was gilded when gold was discovered in Japan as the statue was being completed. The all-pervasive power of the Vairochana Buddha was given extra national significance when the emperor proclaimed that his ancestor, the great Shinto sun deity Amaterasu, had revealed to him that she and the Buddha were one.

On imperial orders, temples and monasteries were built throughout Japan which would be controlled by Todaiji and where the Kegon *sutra*s would be copied and further disseminated. So, while Buddhism was at first the preserve of a Nara elite, the centralization of Buddhist power in the capital gradually resulted in its spread.

TEMPLES ON THE MOUNTAIN

In 784CE the Confucian emperor Kammu left Nara and in 793 established himself in a new capital, Heian-Kyo (City of Peace, modern Kyoto). In the same decade, an idealistic Chinese monk named Saicho (or Dengyo-daishi, 762–822CE) had likewise fled the worldly Buddhist community at Nara for a modest site on Mount Hiei, above Kyoto, which would eventually become the most powerful temple complex of the Heian period (794–1185). The teachings of Saicho's school, Tendai, which followed the older Chinese Tiantai (see pages 121–122), were based on the *Lotus Sutra*. These offered salvation to sincere believers irrespective of rank or learning and became one of the two most influential Buddhist schools of the Heian. This all-embracing

OPPOSITE
A detail of the great bronze Buddha Vairochana at Todaiji temple, Nara. Some lower parts of the present 49-feet (18-m) high statue are from the original 8th-century statue, but damage over the centuries means that most is the work of the Edo period (1603–1868). The statue is housed in the *kondo* of the temple, known as the Daibutsu-den, or Great Buddha Hall, which was rebuilt in the 18th century after it too was destroyed. Even at two-thirds its original 8th-century size, however, the hall remains the world's largest wooden building at 160 feet (49m) high.

universalist generosity was a key aspect of Tendai's success. By the ninth century some Tendai monasteries had incorporated the cult of *Nembutsu*—the invocation of the name of the Buddha (Butsu)—while others had taken up the study of *mandalas*.

Toward the end of the Heian, the monastic populations of Mount Hiei and Kyoto had so increased that there were frequent outbursts of violent rivalry. During the eleventh century, battles between monks of the Tendai and Hosso (Yogachara) school twice led to the destruction of the Tendai Miidera temple.

The Heian also saw the development of another highly popular school, Shingon, which was introduced to Kyoto by Kukai (also called Kobo-daishi, 774–835CE), a Nara aristocrat and monk, following a visit to China in 805. Shingon, deriving from the Chinese *zhen yan* ("true word," Sanskrit *mantra*), emerged from a form of Indian Tantric Buddhism, or Vajrayana, which taught that the cosmic Buddha Vairochana was the source of all phenomena and that all people were capable of realizing their identity with this Buddha in body, speech, and mind through ritual hand gestures (*mudras*), the repetition of mystic syllables (*mantras*), and meditation on *mandalas*, or sacred diagrams.

While Kukai had little interest in or access to the historical Buddha's teachings, Shingon *mudras*, *mantras*, and *mandalas* retained recognizably Indian identities. For example, Kukai insisted on using Sanskrit syllables, both spoken and written, in Shingon *mantras* and *mandalas*. "True words in the original language," he wrote, "possess profound meaning. This changes when the sound is altered. That is why we must go back to the source."

焼香嚴華鳴鐘擊壹

作諸伎樂以七寶器

盛四海水諸仙人衆

各各頂戴授婆羅門

如是及至遍及諸臣

悉巳頂戴傳授與王

時王即以太子頂以

七寶幣而用付之又

擊大敲高聲唱言令

立薩婆悉達以爲太

子介時虛空天龍夜

又人非人等作天伎

樂與口同音讚言善

國立太子時餘八國

我當於如毗羅兜

王亦於是日立太子

RINZAI ZEN: THE WAY OF MEDITATION

The two schools of Zen Buddhism that emerged in Japan during the twelfth century both exemplified movements that would become expressively Japanese while also reaching back to the Dharma as it was practiced in India by the Buddha. The word Zen comes from the Chinese Chan, which in turn derives from the Sanskrit *dhyana*, "meditation." Although many subsequent aspects of Japanese cultural and aesthetic life have, at some point, been influenced by Zen, the practice of Zen itself consists largely of silent, nonritualized sitting meditation (*zazen*), modeled on that of the Buddha Shakyamuni during his enlightenment experience.

ABOVE

A page of the *Illustrated Sutra on Cause and Effect* (*E Inga-kyo*), from Kyoto's Jobon Rendaiji temple. A fine, and rare, example of Nara-period painting, it gives an account of the Buddha's lives, and depicts various episodes. The manuscript served as a model for illustrated handscrolls of the Heian period (794–1185).

LEFT
A painted, lacquered, and gilded
wooden *bodhisattva* mask worn
by temple priests during Gyodo
ceremonies. Derived from Tang-
dynasty China, these enacted the
reception of souls by Amida
(Amitabha) Buddha into paradise.
Kamakura period, 13th century CE.

The earlier of the Zen schools entered Japan during the Kamakura period (1185–1333), following the rise of the Kamakura-based military shogunate, which in 1192 displaced the imperial court in Kyoto after thirty years of clan warfare. Eisai (1141–1215), the Japanese monk who established the first Zen monastery in Kamakura, had studied in the Chinese tradition of Chan Buddhism called Linji (Japanese, Rinzai). Linji/Rinzai based much of its practice on the contemplation of the iconoclastic sayings of its own masters. "If you should meet the Buddha, kill him!" one Chinese master had proclaimed. "Nirvana and *bodhi* [enlightenment] are dead stumps to tie your donkeys to." In other words, genuine Buddhist experience has nothing to do with venerating individuals and images, repeating formulae, or analyzing doctrine. All such practices are mere accretions to the central truth that every human being possesses the same "Buddha-mind"—potential for Buddhahood—as the Buddha himself.

In order to comprehend this, the individual must drop rational and scholarly enquiry and work patiently toward perceiving the Mahayana truth of the "emptiness" (*shunyata*) of all phenomena. This notion is summed up in the brief *Heart Sutra*, a late Sanskrit text of the Prajñaparamita (Perfection of Wisdom) school chanted by most Zen monks daily. It proclaims: "Form is emptiness. Emptiness is form."

Rinzai masters believed students could attain a "sudden realization" (*satori*) of such verbally inexpressible truth by "solving" progressively more difficult *koans* (from Chinese *gong an*)—meditational riddles and conundrums, mostly translated from Chinese. *Koans* encourage states of conscious awareness where rational thought gives way to clear, free intuition of the reality of *shunyata*. In modern times, some of the most famous of these elusive, paradoxical, and often apparently nonsensical sayings—such as "What is the sound of one hand clapping?"—have entered a wider non-Buddhist culture of folklore and hearsay. But Linji/Rinzai *koan* anthologies also contain prose and verse commentaries by later monks which radiate both spiritual insight and literary genius.

A detail of the great bronze statue of Amida Buddha in the grounds of the Kotokuin temple near Kamakura. At more than 37 feet (11m) tall it is Japan's second largest Buddha statue after that at the Todaiji temple in Nara. Cast in 1252, it was originally placed inside a temple hall but has stood in the open since the hall was destroyed by a *tsunami* in the late 15th century. The statue is hollow, enabling worshippers to enter it.

After a period of decline, Rinzai was revitalized through the teachings of Hakuin (1685–1768), who was at once monk, poet, painter, and master calligrapher. Since the time of Eisai, who is also said to have introduced the Japanese to tea drinking, Rinzai Zen has inspired many of the Japanese arts, including the subtleties of the "tea ceremony" and, with the enthusiastic adoption of Zen by Kamakura samurai, Japanese martial arts.

SOTO ZEN: THE PATH OF QUIET DISCIPLINE

Soto, the second major school of Japanese Zen, was adapted from the Chinese Caodong-zong and established in Japan by Dogen Zenji (1200–1253) following four years of study in China. Rinzai was the more institutionally successful during the medieval period, on account of its greater number of urban temples and its standing with the Kamakura shogunate. Soto, which has survived in greater strength into the twenty-first century, was initially smaller, partly because Dogen established monasteries "away from cities and rulers," as the Chinese master Juching had advised him. Repelled, on his return to Japan, by the comfortable lifestyle of some Rinzai monasteries, Dogen chose to teach first at Koshoji temple on the outskirts of his native

A 13th-century ink painting on silk of the *bodhisattva* Jizo (Sanskrit, Kshitigarbha). One of the most popular of Japanese divinities, Jizo is devoted to all who suffer, particularly those in hell, and is the protector of travelers and children. Jizo shrines are abundant in Japan, especially in graveyards—his name is a translation of the Sanskrit and literally means womb (*zo*) of the earth (*ji*).

Kyoto and for the final decade of his life in the remote Eiheiji temple in the region of today's city of Fukui. Here, in seclusion, Dogen composed voluminous writings, from Zen training manuals to the immense *Shobogenzo* (*Treasury of the True Dharma Eye*), a complex spiritual and literary masterwork, unsurpassed in Japanese Zen writing.

Rinzai stressed the value of sudden enlightenment or realization (*satori*) and Soto emphasized both meditation on daily activities and an arduous long-term continuity of *zazen*. However, the basic practice of both schools focuses on *zazen*, and their

aims are also essentially the same: liberation from the
illusion of intrinsic existence, or "self," which would lead
to the comprehension of an absolute reality of "no-self,"
emptiness. But enlightenment was merely the beginning of a
practice in which *satori* must constantly be "polished" or reaffirmed
in zealous continued meditation and, not least, rooted in the
bodhisattva's vow to "save others before realizing your own entry
into the extinction of *nirvana*."

Despite the rigors of Soto discipline as prescribed by
Dogen, it contains a simplicity through which aspirants may
be encouraged not only to achieve knowledge of their own
Buddha-mind, but to become at one with all nature. This
comes, wrote Dogen, when you go "beyond thinking and nonthinking,
good and evil, right and wrong." To achieve "Buddha-mind," the practitioner must, paradoxically, "stop the functions of the mind and give up
the idea of being a Buddha," wrote Dogen in his disconcertingly forthright
manner. But so deep is our delusion that the task is urgent: "Imagine your
head is in flames," he enjoined his disciples. "Now is the time to save it!"

DEPICTING ENLIGHTENMENT: ZEN AND THE ARTS

One of the paradoxes of Zen lay in its zealous theoretical repudiation of
the arts while the same austere energy often generated intense aesthetic
creativity. While Mahayana Sanskrit texts such as the *Heart Sutra*,
Diamond Sutra, and *Lankavatara Sutra* underpinned Zen thought, the
essence of Zen resided in its independence of textual learning and
detachment from symbols. Perhaps the most telling image from the few
Chan artworks to survive is a thirteenth-century scroll by Liang Kai

which depicts Huineng (638–713CE), the celebrated sixth Chan patriarch, tearing up a *sutra*. Self-expression and artistic activity likewise took place in the context of the ascetic enterprise of achieving enlightenment through meditation and the abnegation of self. Uniquely among the many schools of Buddhism, neither Chan nor Japanese Zen kept Buddha images in their monasteries and temples.

The influential example of Huineng presents a further paradox. Enlightenment could never be achieved through the study of texts, and yet this same sixth patriarch proclaimed his own illumination with an exquisite poem—notwithstanding that he was still illiterate and had achieved enlightenment at the sound of bamboo being chopped. This is the "anti-literary" subject of another famous thirteenth-century drawing.

Despite their negativity towards aesthetic ostentation, Zen masters were nonetheless pragmatic. A culture which depended entirely on silent illumination would atrophy and the compassionate embrace of the Mahayana would then reach no one. As with the original Buddhism of India, Chan/Zen was transmitted orally, and the astonishing poetic beauty of *zenkiga*, conversations between Zen masters and students, were recorded in Chinese works such as *The Transmission of the Lamp* and *Blue Cliff Records* which were further distilled in Japanese anthologies such as *The Gateless Gate*. Some leading Zen masters also wrote poetry: major works such as Dongshan Liangjie's *Song of the Jewel Mirror Awareness* represent a spontaneous outflow from the experience of enlightenment, although even within such a masterwork comes the warning that to depict the experience of awakening as literature is to deform it. However, many of the great Japanese *haiku* poets of the seventeenth and eighteenth centuries, such as Basho, Buson, and Issa, wrote from within the same quietly ecstatic experience of insight as their Chinese predecessors. The very brevity of the seventeen-syllable *haiku* suggests a quality of silence from within which the poet's unhindered Zen insight is conveyed.

ZEN VISUAL ARTS

Zen visual arts were often equally expressive of this silent environment and of a balance between passive receptivity and spontaneous engagement with the world. The relationship between poet or painter and his surroundings may be sensed in Chinese landscapes of the Song and Ming dynasties that depict Daoist and Buddhist sages contemplating the mountains, waterfalls, and rivers to which they had retired. Just as the sage meditates amid the dynamic natural changes of which he forms a part, so the artist recreates that relationship between mind and environment in which the viewer is also invited to participate. Japanese versions of this landscape genre were commissioned in the

early fifteenth century by the Muromachi shoguns. Some took the form of *shigajiku* ("poetry paintings") in which scholar-monks inscribed verses within the composition. After long isolation from the mainland during the early Ming dynasty, several Japanese artists of the period reengaged with Chinese Buddhism and aesthetics, including probably the Zen priest Shubun (1423–58), to initiate a genre known as "mind-landscapes." In these, empty landscape spaces were tacitly assumed to represent *shunyata* (emptiness, the void) within which lonely human figures, themselves suffused with *shunyata*, were depicted in meditation. In the fifteenth and sixteenth centuries several other great Buddhist painters—notably Sesshu, Tenyu, Bunsei, and Soami—deployed this haunting counterpoint of idealized landscape and fathomless metaphysical space.

Small-scale studies of flowers, grasses, and birds were also well suited to the art of monochrome ink painting. Compositions with orchids, bamboo, and rock by the fourteenth-century Zen priest and poet Bompo, Ryozen's *White Heron*, and the celebrated *Fresh Turnip* by an anonymous fifteenth-century artist are among the outstanding examples of this genre whose purpose, in part, was to express the energy and reality, or "suchness" (*tatatha*), of even the most insignificant natural phenomena.

In the absence of meditating Buddha icons, the human figure in Zen art was rooted largely in humanistic representation. The Buddha himself, known generally as Shakyamuni ("the sage of the Shakya clan"), appears occasionally in scroll paintings, most commonly in the guise of a poor monk undertaking austerities. Because art was more of a vehicle for expressing and eliciting insight than one for worship, even the two *bodhisattvas* Manjushri (Japanese, Monju) and Samantabhadra (Fugen) are represented respectively as two famous Chan eccentrics of Tang China, Hanshan (Kanzan) and Shide (Jittoku), who are frequent subjects of Chan and Zen illustration. The first Zen patriarch, Bodhidharma (Daruma; see page 121 and illustration, page 160), is also a common subject, depicted with typical Zen irreverence toward the veneration of individuals, no matter how learned or enlightened.

In contrast to these laughing illuminati are the ten mysterious *Ox Herding Pictures*, an earnest series of Zen verses with drawings which trace the progress of a simple man in search of an ox—a symbol for the Buddha-mind—which he believes he has lost. Popular in Song China, Zen monks brought this parable to Japan in the early fourteenth century, and a fine series attributed to Shubun depicts the herder as an

engagingly comic "Everyman" in a semidomesticated "mind-landscape." The eighth picture of the series was always an empty circle, which became a common Zen symbol of the Absolute or of complete enlightenment. Shubun's circle has a lofty, solar character, very different from the quick, rough, black ink versions executed as a single, isolated gesture by many Zen calligraphers.

In contrast to the freedom with which Zen eccentrics and Bodhidharma were portrayed, another genre of humanistic Zen painting was patriarchal portraiture (Japanese, *chinso*), which represented a visual aspect of Zen conversations (*zenkiga*) described earlier. These portraits of masters, personally inscribed by the master himself, were created for disciples who had achieved some measure of enlightenment, to take with them as reminders of their ongoing spiritual bond with a teacher. These portraits were far more than keepsakes. Portraits helped to maintain the continuity of Dharma teaching as it had been understood by both parties, and provided the assurance that the doctrine remained both alive and authentic.

PURE LAND AND NICHIREN

Pure Land Buddhism established itself in China during a time of social and political uncertainty (see pages 118–120). Similarly, Amidism, or devotion to the Buddha Amitabha (Japanese, Amida), was taken up in

The Descent of the Buddha Amida, a hanging scroll painting of 1796 by Kato Nobukiyo (1734–1810). Amida (Amitabha) and the *bodhisattvas* Kannon (Avalokiteshvara) and Seishi or Dai-Seishi (Mahasthamaprapta, an aspect of Vajrapani), descend on a cloud to earth in order to escort the souls of the dead back to Amida's "Pure Land" or paradise. With the growing popularity of Pure Land Buddhism, the depiction of Amida's descent (*raigo*) became a popular genre for Japanese artists. He is often accompanied by the two *bodhisattvas*, who represent the supreme Buddhist qualities of wisdom (Seishi) and compassion (Kannon). This *raigo* painting is entirely composed of thousands of tiny written characters that quote texts from Pure Land *sutras*. In the five years to 1792, Kato Nobukiyo executed 50 scrolls in the same idiom for Ryukoji, a Zen temple in Edo (Tokyo).

LEFT

One of a set of ten hanging scroll paintings depicting the "Six Realms of Being," into any of which a sentient being may be reborn. This first scroll shows a hell scene presided over by Emma, Lord of Hell, with miscreants variously tormented by demons. Edo period, 19th century. In addition to hell, the six realms are those of hungry ghosts, warrior demons, beasts, human beings, and heavenly beings. Only after enlightenment will the soul be released from this cycle. The realm that affords the best opportunity to achieve enlightenment is that of human beings, and the Buddha enjoined his followers to take full advantage of their "precious human birth." Pure Land Buddhism presents a further possibility: a human being who has not attained enlightenment before death may, through devotion to Amitabha, be reborn in Amitabha's Pure Land, a paradise where, free from worldly burdens, one may reach *nirvana*.

A version (detail), from a temple at Okuin, of a much revered historical image—the main icon of Pure Land Buddhism, in fact— known as the *Taima Mandara* from Taimadera temple, Nara, and originally dated to the 8th century. The Buddha Amida (center), flanked by the *bodhisattvas* Kannon (right) and Seishi (left) and attended by many other *bodhisattvas* and heavenly beings, preaches the Dharma within his heavenly palace to those reborn in the Pure Land, who emerge from lotuses in the pond in the foreground. Amida is also shown preaching under two trees, and in pavilions flanking the central area. Panel in pen and ink and gold leaf, 15th century CE.

Japan during the Heian period at a time when many believed that Mappo—the predicted era of Buddhism's decline—had arrived. The dominant Buddhist sect up to this time had been Tendai (see page 151) which had its focus on the saving power of the *Lotus Sutra*. But with Amidism, which Tendai both tolerated and partially incorporated in its wide embrace, came the promise that everyone could reach salvation. This, without ritual or knowledge of scripture, was available to anyone, from educated aristocrat to unlettered peasant, who put their faith in Amida with the *mantra* called the *Nembutsu* (*Namu Amida Butsu*: "I call on you, Amida Buddha").

Amidism reached the peak of its influence during the Kamakura period, through the teachings of the monk Honen (1133–1212) and his disciple Shinran (1173–1263), a lay teacher who claimed that Amida had already forgiven everyone. A beautiful genre of painting (*raigo*), which depicted the descent of Amida, became popular during the Kamakura, and *raigo* scrolls were often hung by the deathbeds of devotees.

In a somewhat rebellious response to institutionalized Tendai and Amidism, the monk Nichiren (1222–82) developed his own sternly prophetic version of devotion to the *Lotus*, in which he prescribed the recitation of the mantra *Namu Myoho-renge-kyo* ("Homage to the *Lotus Sutra*") in preference to the Amidist *Nembutsu*, whose repetition, claimed Nichiren, would lead to hell.

OPPOSITE

A carved ivory *netsuke* or toggle, once used by Japanese men to suspend pouches and containers from their sashes by a silken cord. This 19th-century example depicts peonies and a cloud-wreathed moon. The peony symbolizes health and prosperity, while the prominent moon (*getsu*) emerging from the clouds alludes to the eternal truth of the Dharma that lies behind the obscuration of ignorance. The round shape of the moon, and indeed of the entire *netsuke*, recalls the empty circle of the Zen *Ox Herding Pictures* (see page 165).

BUDDHISM UNDER THE SHOGUNS

The period of the Kamakura shoguns (1185–1333) and their successors in the Muromachi and Momoyama periods (1333–1603), had seen a flourishing of Buddhism, especially of the Zen and Pure Land sects. The final lineage of shoguns, the Tokugawa (1603–1868), closed Japan to overseas contact and, although they continued to adhere to Buddhism, established a new political order based on strict Neoconfucian principles. This order focused more on social control than on Buddhist speculation or an interest in spiritual liberation. Buddhist priests had imported the Neoconfucian texts from China, but the Tokugawa removed Neoconfucianism from the intellectual control of the Buddhist monasteries. The center of religious and philosophical interest in the following centuries lay in practical questions of order and in social issues that dealt with the relationship of the individual to the state, with which Buddhism had seldom been concerned. This, for individual practitioners in the temples and monasteries, was often of no concern. Buddhism continued to exist quietly, and fine religious works of art continued to be produced.

In the 1870s, following the restoration of imperial power and a revival of Shinto as Japan's "national" religion, there was a shortlived backlash against the "foreign" religion of Buddhism, which even saw some looting of temples by zealots. In the late 1880s, however, the government ended such active hostility. While Shinto remained the official state religion until 1945, the historical equilibrium between Japan's two major faiths was restored and persists to the present.

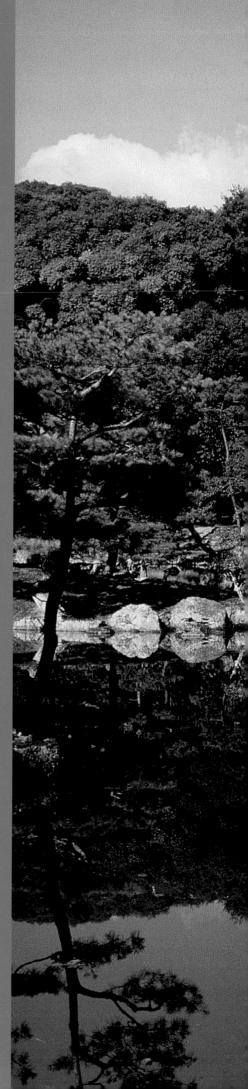

JAPANESE GARDENS

VISIONS OF PARADISE

OPPOSITE
OPPOSITE
The Kinkakuji (Golden Pavilion),
also known as Rokuonji, was
begun in 1397 as part of a
residence for the retired shogun
Ashikaga Yoshimitsu. It was
converted into a Zen temple
after the shogun's death in 1408.
Covered in gold leaf, the Golden
Pavilion also functioned to house
sacred Buddhist relics. Destroyed
by fire in 1950, the pavilion was
rebuilt in 1955.

Four centuries before Zen monks created their
exquisitely austere rock gardens in which gravel
was raked into patterns that alluded to water, the
Japanese garden was already a place in which aesthetic,
social, and meditational pleasure could all be pursued.
Among the first references to formal Japanese gardens is
an anonymous eighth-century poem in praise of the
emperor's Divine Spring Garden in Kyoto. There, "all is
calm and clear. A pure spring bubbles. In the dragon
pond, the sun and moon are reflected."

The symbolism of elements of early Heian gardens has largely been lost. Rocks and wooded islands in
the ponds may have represented aspects of the untamed
Japanese landscape. "Night mooring" stones perhaps
represented seagoing ships, while other stones may have
been determined by Shinto ideas, for rocks and water
were traditionally sacred to spirits.

By the later Heian period, some gardens were
being converted into earthly representations of the
Western Paradise of Amida (Amitabha Buddha). The
aristocratic pleasure park, with its recreational pavilions
assimilated into temple buildings, now provided a fore-
taste of salvation. The first garden transformed in this
way was probably the Byodo-in, just south of Kyoto at
Uji. This was converted from a property of the powerful Fujiwara clan into an Amida paradise garden,
complete with its famous Chinese-style Phoenix Hall.

ZEN GARDENS

To the west of Kyoto, the Saihoji temple provided the site of the first paradise pond garden to be recast, by Muso Soseki in 1339, into a Zen garden as a meditation place for Rinzai monks. Carpeted today by an extraordinary profusion of moss, Saihoji continues to feature an Amida-style pond garden on one level, while the upper garden is in dry landscape "withered mountain-water" style (*karesansui*), in which moving water is represented by dry rocks and gravel. Another of Muso's celebrated gardens was Tenryuji, northeast of Kyoto, which contains a characteristic cluster of features on the western side of a small pond. Most prominent is the "rock island," consisting of seven "mountain" stones, the tallest of which is a tapering vertical which dominates its neighbors, in conformity to Chinese Song-dynasty landscape painting theory. On land behind these stones is a stone bridge and serried dry rocks representing a cascade.

A Rinzai garden that may have taken its shape from Chinese landscape painting is at Daisenin, a subtemple of Daitokuji in northern Kyoto. A small and intense area of this garden offers a perfect example of "withered mountain-water" style, a waterfall in this case simulated by quartz veins in darker rock, while river currents are suggested by raked white gravel. Ryogenin is another subtemple of Daitokuji whose most celebrated feature, attributed to the design of the landscape painter Soami, is an arrangement of small rocks set into a thick rectangular bed of moss.

The dry Zen garden in its simplest, most complete, and most utterly mysterious form is Ryoanji, Kyoto, which consists of fifteen stones set into a rectangle of raked gravel some 100 feet (30m) in length. Probably constructed in the early sixteenth century, Ryoanji may also have been the design of Soami. The dry rock and gravel provide a complete, but ultimately uninterpretable statement of Zen art. Asymmetrical and naturally textured, the rocks present something of the same ideal of material "poverty" (*sabi wabi*) expressed in the roughly-fashioned ceramics used in the tea ceremony (see page 161).

VIETNAM

UNITY IN DIVERSITY

Before the arrival of Buddhism in Vietnam, the religions of the Vietnamese elite combined versions of Confucian and Daoist systems, while, in common with most other Asian societies, the mass of the population was devoted to shamanistic ritual and local spirit cults. It is thought that by ca. 200CE priests from south China had introduced a form of Theravada Buddhism into Vietnam. Theravada established itself particularly strongly in the north of the country, then part of the Chinese empire, at the city of Luy-Lau, north of present-day Hanoi. This consequently became a center for scholarly activity, and several Theravadin *sutras, Jataka* stories, and other canonical texts such as the *Milindapanha (Questions of King Milinda)* were translated here into both Chinese and Vietnamese.

The northern port of Hanoi, the present-day capital, was an important point on the sea route between India and China. In 580CE the Indian monk Vinitaruchi brought a subtle Indian Buddhism of the sort that also traveled to China via the Silk Road and developed into Chan, or Zen (Vietnamese Thien). A second Zen transmission was brought from China in the eighth century by Wu Yantong, and Zen became widely popular owing to its prevalence among the royal elite of the northern kingdom of Dai Viet following its achievement of independence from China in 938CE. Alongside Zen, a *bodhisattva*-focused Buddhism also took root, which evolved into a Pure Land salvationism that was popular among village people and the wider populations of the towns and cities. This is reflected in abundant images of the celestial Buddha Amitabha (known in Vietnam as Adida Phat), the Buddha of the Western Paradise (Pure Land), and his emanation, the *bodhisattva* Avalokiteshvara (Lokeshvara).

Buddhism suffered a decline at the elite level in favor of Confucianism in the wake of a Chinese invasion in the fifteenth century, but underwent something of a revival two centuries later with the introduction of the Linji and Caodong Zen schools from China. This period saw the construction and restoration of numerous temples and monasteries.

Vietnamese Buddhist temples and monastic buildings resemble Chinese ones in their broad outline, but many feature strikingly original departures from Chinese models in terms of layout, structure, and decorative features. For example, many of the sacred buildings of the Ly and Tran dynasties (1054–1400) were constructed on a monumental scale, often with pairs of tall towers up to thirteen stories high. The huge Phat Tich and Dam monasteries were erected on specially leveled areas of mountainside, while Hanoi's unique One Pillar Pagoda, originally erected in 1049, emerges from a pool of water on a single column, like a lotus in blossom—an image representing the emergence from ignorance into enlightenment.

Zen spread to southern Vietnam as the northern kingdom unified the country from the fifteenth century. This region had historically been shared by the Cham and Khmer (Cambodian) peoples, who followed various strands of Mahayana and Hinduism. Elements of Cham decoration also found its way into Vietnamese Buddhist architecture, such as the eagle-like garuda

protector figure of Hindu mythology, alongside other native Vietnamese features such as wave motifs, elephants, lotuses, dragons, and lions.

Buddhism in Vietnam has always been of a remarkably syncretic form, and in the past century other forms of Buddhism have taken root alongside traditional schools such as Zen. Hoahao, established in 1939 and inspired by the vision of the "Healing Buddha of Tay An" on the sacred mountain of That Son ninety years earlier, is popular in the Mekong delta. Another recent school, Cao Dai ("High Abode"), started in the mid-1920s and combines all the great religions, including Buddhism, to promote mutual understanding among peoples. Cao Dai represents the ultimate in the Vietnamese genius for syncretic religious possibilities.

LEFT

An elaborately robed sculpture of Amitabha Buddha in gilded lacquer on wood. The Buddha sits meditating in the lotus position, his hands in *dhyanamudra* (meditation posture). His tight curls and long ears conform to the iconography of the Indian sculptural tradition. From Hanoi, northern Vietnam, 18th or 19th century.

RIGHT

Avalokiteshvara, the *bodhisattva* of mercy, in his eight-armed form. In attempting to reach all who suffered, Avalokiteshvara found two arms insufficient. The Buddha Amitabha thereupon gave him eight with which to rescue those in need. Another legend attributes 1,000 arms to the *bodhisattva*. An 18th-century gilded and lacquered polychrome figure from Hanoi.

chapter 5

THE HIMALAYAS AND MONGOLIA

THE VAJRAYANA TRADITION

OPPOSITE

The *bodhisattva* Maitreya, the future Buddha, is portrayed here in a colossal gilded statue at Thikse monastery in Ladakh, a culturally Tibetan region of northern India. Maitreya is believed to reside in a heaven called Tushita, awaiting the "Dark Age," a time when he must descend to earth to restore the Dharma.

TIBET

THE BELL AND THE THUNDERBOLT

Tibet was among the last of the Asian lands to come into contact with Buddhism, which had no significant presence there before the seventh century CE. But nowhere else was the Dharma more thoroughly assimilated into the national cultural identity. Even today, after a turbulent half-century in which Tibetan religious traditions have faced challenges ranging from a Maoist attempt at total annihilation to a policy of limited tolerance under strict state control, the Buddhist roots of Tibet remain strong. Uniquely among Buddhist nations, Tibet was until recently ruled by a king who was not only a senior *lama* (teacher) of a monastic lineage but also universally acknowledged by his subjects as the incarnation of the great *bodhisattva* of compassion, Avalokiteshvara. The current holder of this office, the Fourteenth Dalai Lama, has lived in exile since 1959 but is still acknowledged by Tibetans both within and outside the country as their nation's spiritual leader.

ART AND BELIEF

Even today, religion is marked on the very landscape of Tibet, with countless stupas (*chörtens*), prayer flags, and wayside shrines denoting places of spiritual significance, and painted stones bearing the *mantra* of Avalokiteshvara—*Om Mani Padme Hum*—lining even the remotest mountain paths. In a country where, within living memory, one-quarter of the male population were once monks, and where, uniquely in the Buddhist world, the monastic community always took precedence over the secular powers, it is unsurprising that almost all artworks were made for a religious purpose. These range from tiny molded clay *tsha-tshas* (votive talismans) and cloth prayer-flags block-printed with sacred prayers and *mantras*, to

exquisite wood and metal sculptures of Tibet's innumerable deities in all their forms and attributes and brilliantly coloured *thangkas* (devotional paintings on cloth that are used as the focus of meditation and other rituals). The latter include sacred cosmic diagrams known as *mandalas*, which are also produced in various other forms (see pages 198–201) .

The elaborate rites and ceremonies of Tibetan Buddhism require a host of smaller sacred implements that include the miniature bell (*ghanta*) and "diamond thunderbolt" (*vajra*) that are used in Tantric rituals, and elaborately decorated musical instruments. One common implement unique to Tibetan Buddhism is the magical ritual dagger (*purbhu*) used to avert evil forces.

SUBDUING THE DEMONS

According to Tibetan histories, Buddhism first took hold in Tibet during the reign of King Songtsen Gampo (died ca. 650CE), a ruler whose ancestors came from the Yarlung Valley. Songsten Gampo succeeded in unifying Tibet and although he was not himself a Buddhist he had two Buddhist queens, one Chinese and one Nepalese, who are said to have ordered the building of Tibet's

RIGHT

Constructed in the 17th century
by the "Great Fifth" Dalai Lama,
the Potala palace towers above
the Tibetan capital of Lhasa. It
was built to represent the sacred
Mount Potalaka, the home of the
bodhisattva Avalokiteshvara, of
whom each Dalai Lama is said
to be an incarnation. Both a
monastery and a fortress, until
1959 the Potala was the seat
of the Dalai Lamas and of the
Tibetan government. In the
foreground is the rooftop of the
Jokhang, the most sacred temple
in the whole of Tibet, founded
in the 7th century CE by Bhrikuti,
the Nepalese queen of King
Songtsen Gampo. The gilded
"Dharma Wheel" flanked by
two deer (representing the
Buddha's first sermon in the
deer park at Sarnath) was
added in 1927. The Jokhang
attracts pilgrims from all over
Tibet who come to offer devotion
to an image of the Buddha
known as the Jowo Rinpoche.
Said originally to have been
made in India, it was brought
to Tibet by Weng Chen, Songtsen
Gampo's Chinese queen, and has
been at the Jokhang since 650CE.

OPPOSITE

A manuscript of the so-called *Tibetan Book of the Dead*, in Tibetan the *Bardo Thodol* (*Liberation through Hearing in the Transitional State*), which is recited to a dead or dying person. The illustrations depict wrathful deities that the consciousness may encounter in the transition between death and rebirth. A higher form of birth, or even awakening and *nirvana*, will be achieved if such beings are correctly recognized as simply aspects of the self.

FOLLOWING PAGES

Samye, Tibet's oldest monastery, founded in the 8th century CE by the Indian masters Shantarakshita and Padmasambhava. The complex takes the form of a huge cosmic diagram, or *mandala*. The central multistoried temple—said to combine Tibetan, Indian, and Chinese styles—represents Meru, or Sumeru, the mountain at the center of the universe.

first Buddhist temple, the great Jokhang in Lhasa, Tibet's most revered shrine (see pages 184–185). The Nepalese queen, Bhrikuti, is said to have seen Tibet as a great demoness, who could be subdued only by building temples on her body. To this end several other Buddhist temples were built around the country; the Jokhang reputedly stands on the demoness's heart, originally a small lake.

It was around this time that a Tibetan script was first developed, based on the alphabetic scripts of north India. Tibetan manuscripts, often exquisitely illustrated and with elaborately carved wooden covers, retained the traditional horizontal form of the palm-leaf that developed in India and Sri Lanka (see pages 70–71)

A century or so later, King Trisong Detsen (756–ca.780CE) invited two noted Indian teachers, Shantarakshita and Padmasambhava, to establish Tibet's first monastery near the Tsangpo (Brahmaputra) River at Samye (see pages 188–189). Here, an eighth-century stela records the king's vow to uphold the Dharma.

Padmasambhava is revered by Tibetans simply as Guru Rinpoche ("Blessed Teacher"), the first of Tibet's great Buddhist saints and the founder of the Nyingmapa, the oldest of Tibet's four main monastic schools (the Nyingmapa, Kagyupa, Sakyapa, and Gelukpa). Legend has it that he too was obliged to overcome powerful forces in order to build Samye, and it is said that the old

ༀ་ཨོཾ༔ ༔འཕྱོཿཕྲ་ཉོཾ༔ ཀུན
བཟང་ཆེ་མ་ཆེ་ག་ཨ་བྷེ་ར་ཡི༔

ཆོས་པ་དགའ་རབ༔

ༀ་ཨོཾ༔ ༔ཚོགས་ག་ས་ང་རྡ༔ ར་ཁ་བ
ར་ས་བ་རྒྱ་འདུ་ས་བ་འཆོ་ག་ས་རུམ༔
ལ༔ སུ་ས་བ་ས་ཁྱ་ག་འཚོ་ལ་བ་ར་

གཅིག་འད་དགར་སྟུ༔

ABOVE

Represented as part eagle and
part human, the garuda is of
Indian origin and is revered
in many parts of the Buddhist
world as a protector against
malign forces. It is often shown
devouring a snake and in Tibet
may be depicted protecting the
throne of the Buddha. Gilded
wood, 19th century. (See also
pages 96 and 182.)

deities and demons of Tibet were so awed by his powers that from that time they
acknowledged the supremacy of Buddhism. Some became assimilated into the new
religion as Dharmapalas ("Dharma Protectors"), and Tibetan art is replete with depictions of these wrathful and terrifying beings, often festooned with severed heads and
wielding blood-filled cups made from human skulls. Many are important in Tantric
practice as symbols of the "anger without hatred" with which the practitioner must
confront disturbing forces within the mind, such as greed, hatred, and delusion.

From ca. 840CE the Yarlung monarchy succumbed to civil war and, without
the support of a unified state, Buddhism underwent a decline to the extent that it sub-

sequently had to be revived by scholars and *siddhas* (adepts). Tibetans traveled to Nalanda and other great centers of Buddhist learning in India, and Indian teachers made the long hazardous trek over the Himalayas to Tibet. The arrival of Atisha (982–1054) from eastern India in 1042 marks what Tibetans call the "Second Propagation" of Buddhism. Atisha's disciples established the Kadampa school, from which the Gelukpa later evolved. A prominent Gelukpa *lama*, the Dalai Lama, effectively ruled Tibet as head of state until the 1950s.

THE DIAMOND THUNDERBOLT

The main transmission route of Buddhism to Tibet from the seventh to twelfth centuries was from the great Buddhist centers of north and northeast India. The Buddhism current in this region at the time was Mahayana, together with its esoteric branch, known as Tantra or Vajrayana, the "Vehicle of the Diamond Thunderbolt." Tibetan Buddhism reflects both mainstream and esoteric strands of Mahayana. Mainstream practices and doctrines, as derived from the Mahayana *sutras*, were aimed at the gradual pursuit of enlightenment through the cultivation of compassion (*karuna*) and wisdom (*prajña*), perhaps over hundreds of lifetimes. Vajrayana, on the other hand, asserted that there was the "rapid path" to Buddhahood in a single lifetime, based on tantras or "secret teachings" said to have been given by the Buddha and passed down through eighty-four *Mahasiddhas* or Great Adepts.

Tantric practice involves working closely with a learned teacher (*lama*), who instructs the devotee

This copper and silver incense burner bears the Buddhist "Eight Auspicious Emblems" that appear widely in Tibetan art: the royal parasol (the Buddha); the fishes (happiness and utility); the vase (plenty); the lotus (purity); the conch (turning toward Dharma); the infinite knot (endless rebirth); the "victory banner" atop Mt. Meru; and the wheel of Dharma. The lid is surmounted by another Dharma wheel between two deer, denoting the Buddha's first sermon at Sarnath.

through a series of intense and often highly elaborate spiritual practices aimed at cultivating wisdom and compassion. Such practices include meditation on a host of Buddhas and deities, some fierce or "wrathful," which at the most profound level are understood as representing aspects of the human psyche. These divine beings are depicted in elaborate detail on *thangkas*. The supreme Tantric goal of uniting wisdom and compassion is specifically symbolized in images referred to as *yab-yum*, depicting a male deity (compassion) and female deity (wisdom) in sexual union.

INFLUENTIAL NEIGHBORS

It appears that Chinese Buddhist influences were also present in the country in the earliest years, and there is said to have been a great debate at Samye in 792–794CE between Chinese monks of the Chan school (see pages 120–121) and Indian monks advocating the more gradual path to enlightenment. The Chinese monks are said to have lost the argument, from which time Tibetan Buddhism became firmly oriented toward India.

However, the rejection of Chinese doctrines may have been motivated by politics as much as religion, aimed at reducing the influence of Tibet's powerful neighbor. If Chinese doctrinal influences were excluded, Chinese styles did subsequently leave their mark on Tibetan art, particularly from the thirteenth century, when both China and Tibet were dominated by the Mongol (Yuan) dynasty, which practiced the Tibetan form of Buddhism. A Sino-Tibetan style evolved that received renewed impetus under China's last dynasty, the Manchu (Qing), who were also adherents of Tibetan Buddhism.

The influence of Tibet's southern neighbor, Nepal, is also evident in certain aspects of Tibetan art. It is most noticeable in the style of the Tibetan stupa, or *chörten*, particularly the tall spire-like finial and, in some cases, the painted Buddha-eyes that look down on the devotee from each side of the *harmika*, the box-like component between the dome and the spire.

ENLIGHTENED BEINGS

Tibetan Buddhism embraces the most elaborate array of sacred beings to be found in any Buddhist tradition. Images of celestial Buddhas, *bodhisattvas*, fierce protector deities, great teachers (*lamas*), and famous Indian and Tibetan adepts (*siddhas*) are represented in almost every medium, as are scenes from the lives of the Buddha Shakyamuni and ancient Tibetan legends. Complementing such subjects is a rich and complex system of sacred symbolism: pure decoration is relatively rare in Tibetan art, and virtually every detail and color of a *thangka* possesses some religious significance.

A key aspect of the Mahayana is its emphasis on compassion. A number of the Buddha's disciples are said to have attained enlightenment, and

RIGHT

The goddess Tara appears in this *thangka* painting in her two most common forms. Beneath Green Tara (center) are White Tara (left) and Avalokiteshvara, from whose compassionate tears Tara was born. At the top are three Gelukpa lamas, including the school's founder, Tsong Khapa (center).

these became revered as *arhats* or "worthy ones." However, according to Mahayana theory, the *arhats* sought to show only by their own example that the Dharma was the correct way to *nirvana*, but otherwise did not demonstrate the compassion toward all suffering beings that would have made them Buddhas. So, while worthy of reverence, the *arhats* were spiritually inferior to *bodhisattvas*, who stand on the verge of Buddhahood after countless lifetimes helping others in acts of self-sacrifice.

Consequently, the veneration of a host of *bodhisattvas* is central to Tibetan Buddhism. As in other Mahayana traditions, the most popular is Avalokiteshvara (Chenrezi), the "Lord Who Looks Down" in compassion on suffering beings. He has an added significance in Tibet as the nation's patron deity, physically incarnate in the Dalai Lama, and indeed ancient Tibetan legend claims that the first Tibetan people were the offspring of a fierce goddess and a monkey that was an emanation of Avalokiteshvara. The *bodhisattva* resided on Mount Potalaka in southern India, of which the Potala Palace in Lhasa is a representation (see pages 184–185). He is often depicted in eleven-headed and eight-armed form, symbolizing his eternal vigilance and preparedness to help relieve suffering.

Other popular *bodhisattvas* include Manjushri, the lord of wisdom, who takes many forms but is often depicted wielding the "sword of discrimination" to slice through delusion and attachment. Maitreya, the Buddha of the future age, sits in

ABOVE

Manjushri, the *bodhisattva* of transcendent wisdom, wields the "sword of discrimination," with which he is said to cut through the roots of ignorance. He also holds a sacred book denoting wisdom. Bronze inlaid with silver, copper, and semiprecious stones, 12th century.

"Western" manner on a stool or throne, ready to rise at the world's time of need at some future point when the Dharma has decayed. Also very widely revered by Tibetans is the goddess Tara (Dölma), the female manifestation of Avalokiteshvara, who is depicted as a perpetually young woman of sixteen. She has some twenty-one forms, of which the most common are Green Tara and White Tara.

Each *bodhisattva* is regarded as a manifestation of one of the five "celestial" or "cosmic" Buddhas, who embody aspects of the supreme wisdom of the Buddha and his teachings, and collectively constitute Adibuddha, "Primordial Buddha," the Absolute or

supreme truth that is beyond the world of phenomena. Avalokiteshvara, for example, is an emanation of Amitabha, the Buddha of Infinite Radiance, and lord of the Western Paradise or Pure Land (see page 118–119). The celestial Buddhas are employed in Tantric practice and represent aspects of the psyche; they are also linked to the five elements, the five senses, and the five principal energy centers of the body, in the feet, navel, heart, mouth, and head. The supreme Adibuddha is depicted in different symbolic form by each of the main Tibetan schools, contributing to the uniquely rich and elaborate religious imagery and symbolism that characterizes Tibetan art.

THE MANDALA
THE MOUNTAIN OF THE MIND

One of the most remarkable subjects of Tibetan art is the cosmic diagram, or *mandala.* It comes in a wide variety of media, from small woodblock-printed images on paper and elaborate paintings on cloth, to three-dimensional forms ranging from wooden and metal models to entire buildings, such as the Kumbum at Gyantse and the monastery of Samye. It is also created in more ephemeral media such as sand, clay, and rice. There is even a hand gesture, the *mandala-mudra,* in which the fingers are intertwined to form a *mandala* as an offering gesture.

Usually consisting basically of a circle within a square, the *mandala* represents both the macrocosm of the universe and the microcosm of the individual devotee, and as such it is a key tool in the Tantric path to enlightenment, serving as a guide to mental transformation. In Tantric meditational practice, the individual devotee visualizes the *mandala* and the host of deities residing within it as representing his or her own

mind. The deities visualized are not perceived as real physical beings but as manifestations of wisdom and compassion, and the practitioner aims ultimately to become as one with these qualities. The Tantric path is a difficult one and culminates in advanced esoteric practices that involve imagining oneself as the deity at the heart of the *mandala,* the embodiment of wisdom and compassion—an enlightened being.

The deity at the heart of the *mandala* will be the *yidam* or "personal deity" chosen for a Tantric pupil by an experienced *lama.* There are three types of deity, "peaceful," "wrathful," and "semiwrathful," and which deity is chosen will depend on how the *lama* perceives the student's own personality and psychology. As one Buddhist

The monastery of Gyantse is dominated by the extraordinary pyramid-like temple known as the Kumbum, constructed in the form of a huge, three-dimensional *mandala*. The temple contains more than 70 individual chapels, each filled with images of Buddhist deities. At the top of the temple (the center of the *mandala*) is a shrine room containing an image of Vajradhara, the Gelukpa form of the supreme Adi Buddha (see page 197). The Kumbum was consecrated in 1463, when Gyantse was the center of a small but flourishing principality. The "all-seeing eyes" and the spire-like finial show the influence of the Nepalese artists who may have worked on the temple.

writer has put it, "one's *yidam* represents one's own particular expression of Buddha-nature, and therefore becomes a means by which one can manifest this nature."

VISIONS OF THE GODS

The best-known form of the *mandala* is that depicted in great detail on Tibetan sacred scroll hangings, or *thangkas*. Highly colorful and intricate, such *mandalas* depict a single deity at the center, such as one of the five cosmic Buddhas (see pages 196–197) whose qualities and symbolism may be the focus of the devotee's meditation at a particular stage of their spiritual progress. Surrounding the central deity are other sacred beings, within a square enclosure "wall" with four gates oriented to the four directions. This image, which represents the mountain at the center of the cosmos, is in turn surrounded by a series of circles adorned with various sacred symbols, such as *vajras* (ritual thunderbolts) and lotus petals. Outside the circles there may be a great array of further sacred figures, often famous adepts (*siddhas*) and protector deities.

Among the most remarkable *mandalas* are those painstakingly created from colored sand and employed in Tantric initiation ceremonies. Once the ceremony is over, the *mandala*—which may have taken several weeks to create—is simply swept away, a reminder of the impermanence of all phenomena.

THE UNBROKEN TRADITION

TIBETAN BUDDHISM OUTSIDE TIBET

Along the southern fringes of the Himalayas are a number of historically and culturally Tibetan regions which have ended up within the frontiers of present-day India and Nepal, or, in the unique case of Bhutan, have retained political independence from their larger neighbors. In these often remote mountain areas Buddhists have maintained their ancient Tibetan religious and artistic traditions to the present day, uninterrupted by the calamities that beset their cultural homeland from the mid-twentieth century. In addition, Tibetan Buddhism is practiced far from the Himalayas in Mongolia, a region with close historical ties to Tibet.

THE TIBETANS OF INDIA AND WESTERN NEPAL

Ladakh, now mostly part of the Indian state of Jammu and Kashmir, was an independent Tibetan kingdom until its annexation by Jammu in 1834 and subsequent incorporation into British India. Its numerous monasteries (*gompas*), such as those at Alchi, Lamayuru, and Thikse, belong to three main Tibetan schools, the Gelukpa, Kagyupa, and Drukpa (a subschool of the Kagyupa). The temples of Alchi, near the Ladakhi capital of Leh, are among the earliest Tibetan monuments to survive anywhere; founded ca. 1200, Alchi is noted for its magnificent wall paintings and carved

BELOW

The Pala kingdom of northeastern India was an important source of influence on Tibetan Buddhism and many Tibetans studied at its great monastic seats of learning, Nalanda and Vikramashila. Atisha, the 11th-century reviver of Tibetan Buddhism (see page 191) may have been abbot of Vikramashila. This detail of a Pala palm-leaf manuscript shows a Vajrayana (Tantric) Buddhist deity and dates to the reign of King Ramapala (ruled ca. 1082–1124), a period when Pala influence on Tibetan art was at its peak.

woodwork. Thikse, founded more than five centuries ago, rises imposingly on a hill above the Indus River valley. It is home to an important library and also houses a famous modern statue of Maitreya, the Buddha of the future.

The Indian state of Himachal Pradesh, to the south of Ladakh, is also home to traditional Tibetan populations, as well as many refugees from Tibet proper. The region includes Dharamsala, the seat of the Dalai Lamai and the Tibetan government in exile. Another ancient Tibetan kingdom, Sikkim, between Nepal and Bhutan, was independent until its annexation by India in 1975. Its monastic sites include Rumtek, where a new monastery was built in traditional Tibetan style in the 1960s for the Sixteenth Karmapa, the exiled head of the Karma Kagyupa order. An older Kagyu monastery, founded in the seventeenth century, stands nearby.

Western Nepal has three main areas of Tibetan culture, Dolpo, Mustang, and the Sherpa region. Mustang, an old Tibetan principality, has numerous *gompas*; near

Luri *gompa* are some remarkable decorated cave temples dating from the thirteenth or fourteenth centuries and known to the outside world only since the 1990s. Since the 1950s Tibetan Buddhists have also constituted a sizeable presence in the Kathmandu Valley, Nepal's cultural heartland (see page 209).

BHUTAN: THE LAND OF THE THUNDER DRAGON

The name Bhutan means "End of Tibet," and, with the exception of India's Darjeeling valley to its south, this small Himalayan kingdom forms the southernmost region of historical Tibet. Today it is the only independent Himalayan nation where the majority of the inhabitants practice a form of Tibetan Buddhism. Buddhism has been the predominant religion here since the seventh century, and since the seventeenth century the most powerful school has been the Drukpa, a subschool of the Kagyu, traditionally powerful in eastern and southeastern Tibet. The Drukpa traces its foundation to the Tibetan master Ling Repa (1128–89), founder of Ralung monastery 250 miles (400km) south of Lhasa, not far from the present border with Bhutan. The next largest school is the older Nyingma school.

In form and style, traditional Bhutanese Buddhist art and architecture closely resemble those of Tibet. Frescoes and paintings of *thangkas* and *mandalas* are among the chief subjects of Bhutanese religious art, together with figures of Buddhas, deities, and sacred persons finely crafted of wood, stone, bronze, and precious stones. Bhutanese architecture—only building in traditional styles is permitted—employs wooden construction techniques involving no use of nails. As in Tibet, the chief forms of religious building are monasteries, temples, *dzongs* (fortified monasteries), and *chörtens* (*stupas*). Also as in Tibet, Bhutanese *chörtens* commemorate the Buddha and deceased holy people and also serve as talismans at places deemed to contain great and possibly dangerous spiritual power, such as places where roads or rivers meet. As well as the usual Tibetan type of *chörten* there are numerous examples resembling those of Nepal.

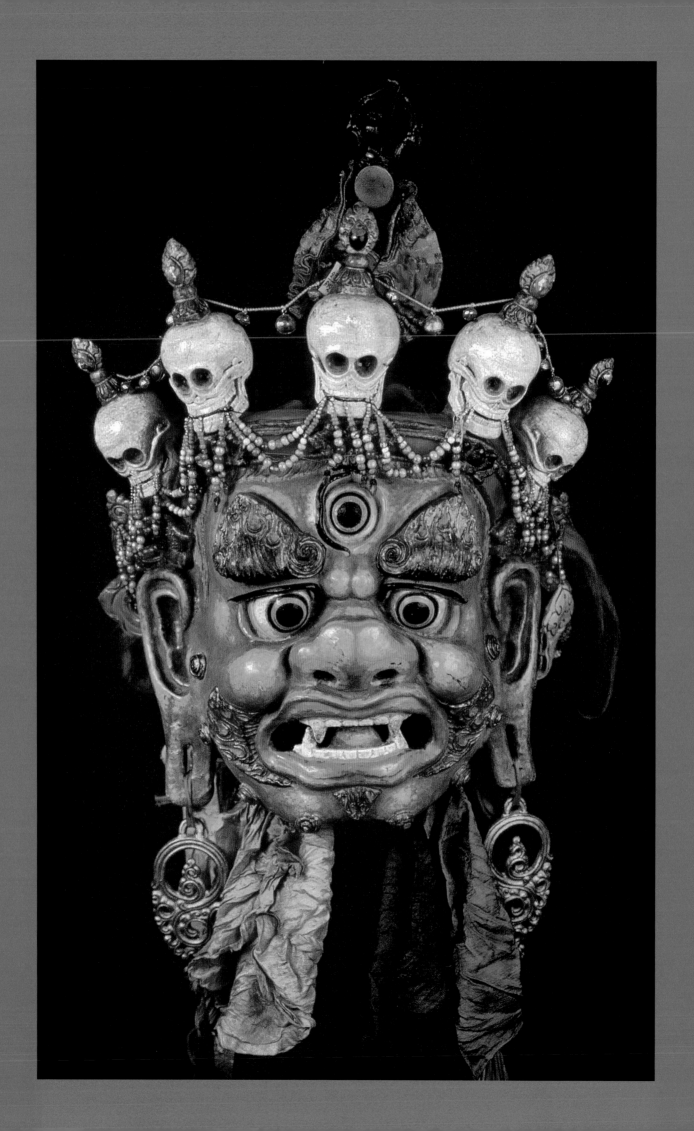

MONGOLIA: THE DHARMA IN THE LAND OF THE KHANS

Outside Tibet proper and other historically Tibetan lands, the most important region to adopt Tibetan Buddhism was Mongolia. According to Chinese sources, Chinese Buddhist monks were present among the Mongols as early as the fourth century CE, and there is evidence for later contacts along the Silk Road. However, it was the connections between the Mongols and the hierarchs of Tibet that proved decisive. In 1244 the head lama of the Shakyapa, then Tibet's dominant school, was appointed regent of the Mongol ruler, Gödän Khan, in return for submitting to Mongol sovereignty. Gödän's successor, Kublai Khan (1215–94), who founded China's Yuan (Mongol) dynasty (1279–1368), converted to Tibetan Buddhism, but the religion became more widespread outside the Mongol aristocracy only after Sonam Gyatso (1543–1588), a senior Gelukpa lama, visited Altan Khan in 1578. The Mongol leader was so impressed with the lama that he gave him the Mongolian title of "Dalai," meaning "ocean (of wisdom)." Mongolia became a bastion of the Gelukpa school, and a century later the Mongols helped Ngawang Losang (1617–82), the "Great Fifth" Dalai Lama, to establish himself and his successors as Tibetan heads of state.

The Mongols broadly followed Tibetan monastic and artistic forms, with local differences, such as peripatetic lamas not tied to a particular monastery. As in Tibet, Mongolian Buddhism suffered under twentieth-century communist regimes. However, in the Mongolian Republic at least, there are signs today of remarkable revival.

ABOVE

Stupas commemorating notable lamas at Mongolia's Erdeni Dzuu monastery, founded in 1586. After Mongolia became the world's second communist state in 1921, all but one of its 600 monasteries were destroyed or secularized. Erdeni Dzuu is one of the 200 or so revived and restored since the end of communist rule in 1990.

OPPOSITE

A 19th-century papier-mâché mask used in the traditional Mongolian New Year Tsam (Tibetan, Cham) dances, in which dancers assumed the roles of Buddhist deities to ward off evil. Suppressed under communism, the Tsam tradition is today being revived by elderly monks who survived decades of persecution.

NEPAL

HOMELAND OF THE BUDDHA

Although India was the place where the Buddha gained enlightenment, taught, and died, it was in present-day southern Nepal that he was born in the sixth or fifth century BCE, in a small princely state in the foothills of the Himalayas. As in Sri Lanka and elsewhere, Nepalese tradition claims that the Dharma first came to the land of its founder's birth in the third century BCE, as part of the missionary activity of the Mauryan emperor Ashoka. However, the Buddha's Nepalese birthplace, Lumbini, may have drawn Buddhist pilgrims well before Ashoka erected a pillar there commemorating his own pilgrimage ca. 254BCE.

Ashoka's pillar still stands on the site of the Lumbini grove, which was abandoned following the decline of Buddhism in India, to be rediscovered only in the late nineteenth century. As well as the pillar, other remains discovered included a brick temple dedicated to Maya, the Buddha's mother. This temple had been built over the foundations of an earlier monument, possibly dating to Ashoka's reign. In the city of Patan (Lalitpur), adjacent to Kathmandu and the cultural center of Nepal until the sixteenth century, stand the remains of four ancient stupas—one at each of the cardinal points—that are also traditionally attributed to Ashoka. Other smaller stupas found in many of the Kathmandu Valley's monastic courtyards are still referred to as "Ashoka *chaityas*" (stupas) today. These attributions cannot be verified with certainty, but the large stupas do have the typical hemispherical dome of the oldest Indian stupas.

THE KATHMANDU VALLEY

The modern kingdom of Nepal encompasses a 500-mile (800km) strip of the Himalaya and its southern foothills fringing the Ganges basin. However, its cultural heartland, and most populous region, has always been the central

Kathmandu Valley, where Hinduism and Buddhism have coexisted for at least two millennia. Until 1769, when it was annexed by Gurkha rulers from further west, it was primarily this region that the name "Nepal" referred to. The seventh-century Chinese scholar and pilgrim Xuanzang learnt that the Kathmandu Valley was home to thousands of Buddhist monks of the Mahayana and other schools of Indian Buddhism. By the third or fourth centuries CE Buddhism flourished in particular among the Newars, an ethnic group speaking a Tibeto-Burmese language whose ancestors had migrated to the valley from the north or northeast in the distant past. By the time of the early Malla kings (ca. 1200–1480), the Newar minority occupied a prominent place in Nepal's overwhelmingly Hindu society, and Newari Buddhism had come increasingly under the influence of late Indian Tantric Buddhism (Vajrayana).

After Buddhism declined in India, Newari doctrine and practice was increasingly influenced by the Hinduism of the majority, especially Shaivite (Shiva-centered) Tantrism. The result, over the centuries, was a form of Mahayana Buddhism that is

ABOVE

A *mandala* of the cosmic Buddha Vairochana (detail). The dominant reds and blues and rich use of foliage motifs are characteristic of the Newari style. Early 19th century, Nepal or possibly Tibet.

OPPOSITE

Queen Maya gives birth to Siddhartha as she leans against a tree in the Lumbini grove. The future Buddha can be seen emerging from her right side. Brass, copper, and semiprecious stones; Nepal, early 19th century.

similar to Tibetan Buddhism, characterized by an emphasis on ritual, the cult of the celestial *bodhisattva* Avalokiteshvara, and on a large and elaborate pantheon of Buddhist saviors and divine protectors. On the other hand, unlike Tibetan Buddhists, Newari Buddhists also conformed to their Hindu rulers in accepting a caste-based social stratification, headed by the two levels of priests (*vajracharyas*, or Tantric "diamond masters," and *shakya-bhikshus*, or "Shakya monks," in reference to the Buddha's clan, the Shakyas). Newari Buddhist priests are permitted to marry and live with their families in monasteries, which consequently often expanded greatly over the centuries to accommodate priestly households.

THE ART OF NEPALESE BUDDHISM

Nepalese monasteries are generally focused on a two-story structure around a central courtyard, a form adopted from the monasteries of northeast India. Beyond the entrance gateway (*torana*), with its two protector deities, the Hindu god Ganesh and the Tantric defender Mahakala, are stupa shrines. In the temple facing the entrance are typically, on the ground level, Buddhas such as Shakyamuni, the eastern Buddha Akshobhya, or Maitreya; on the upper floors are shrines to the esoteric Tantric deities such as Chakrasamvara or Akash Yogini. Nepalese stupas are generally hemispherical, after Indian models, with the striking pair of "all-seeing eyes" painted

on each side of the square *harmika* below the spire. This feature was borrowed by some Tibetan temples, such as the Kumbum at Gyantse (see pages 200–201), on which Nepalese artisans are believed to have worked.

In addition to the stupa there is a distinct type of Nepalese shrine with multi-tiered roofs, each roof differing in size from the one above and with overhanging eaves supported on carved and decorated wooden struts. Such shrines, which are built on a square plan and may be either Buddhist, like the Golden Temple in Patan, or Hindu, like the Nyatapola in Bhaktapur, are commonly referred to as "pagodas" and indeed have been claimed as the models for the Buddhist pagodas of China and elsewhere in the Far East.

Some of the most striking Nepalese Buddhist art is found in book illustrations, since Newari scholars and artisans copied many of the Sanskrit Buddhist texts that survive today. The illustrations to these often possess a fluency and dynamism that bring to mind, in appearance as well as quality, the carvings at Sañchi and the magnificent murals at Ajanta (see pages 46–49 and 50–51). Nepalese manuscript painting affords a glimpse of the rich tradition of Indian Buddhist painting, of which Ajanta is a rare survival. Other genres of Nepalese painting are related to specific rituals such as lamp-lighting and life-cycle rites connected with childhood and old age.

In addition to the Mahayana-Vajrayana Buddhism of the Newars, forms of Tibetan Buddhism are also practiced among the indigenous ethnic Tibetan populations of Nepal's northern frontier regions such as Mustang and Dolpo, and among the Sherpa ethnic group. Buddhism in Nepal is also very vigorous and active today among the sizeable Tibetan minority that has taken up residence in the Kathmandu Valley since the Chinese occupation of Tibet in the 1950s. This community has around 1,200 Tibetan-style monasteries representing all the major Tibetan schools. There is also a growing Theravada reformist movement, whose art is borrowed from Burma, Thailand, and Sri Lanka.

GLOSSARY

All terms are Sanskrit unless stated. The following abbreviations are used:

B	Burmese	P	Pali
C	Chinese	S	Sanskrit
J	Japanese	Si	Sinhala
Kh	Khmer	Th	Thai
K	Korean	T	Tibetan
M	Mongolian	V	Vietnamese

abhidharma (P. *abhidhamma*) Advanced philosophical teachings. See also *Tripitaka*.

Amitabha (C. Amituo, J. Amida etc.) Compassionate celestial Buddha of the Western Paradise.

anatman (P. *anatta*) "No self," absence of self or ego: one of the Trilakshana (Three Characteristics of Existence), according to the Buddha. See also *anitya, duhkha*.

anitya (P. *anicca*) Impermanence: one of the Trilakshana (Three Characteristics of Existence), according to the Buddha. See also *anatman, duhkha*.

arahat (P. *arhat*) An adept of early Buddhist history who has attained *nirvana*. *Arhat*s are of particular importance in Theravada Buddhism, but are also depicted in Mahayana art. See also *bodhisattva*.

ashura A demon figure, which entered Buddhism from Hindu myth and is often represented in Indian sculpture.

Avalokiteshvara The *bodhisattva* of compassion, a major deity of the Mahayana, known as Guanyin in China, Kwannon or Kannon in Japan, Chenrezi in Tibet, Lokeshvara in Southeast Asia, etc.

bhikshu (P. *bhikkhu*) A Buddhist monk; a celibate follower of the Buddha: literally "beggar."

bhikshuni (P. *bhikkhuni*) A Buddhist nun.

bodhi The experience of enlightenment, awakening.

Bodhi Tree The pipal tree (*Ficus religiosa*) beneath which the Buddha attained enlightenment at Bodhgaya (present day Bihar province, India).

bodhisattva (P. *bodhisatta*) "Enlightenment being." In Theravada, one on the path to Buddhahood, a future Buddha. In the Mahayana, a *bodhisattva* is a being who, motivated by compassion (*karuna*), strives for the attainment of full and perfect Buddhahood for the benefit of all sentient beings. Some *bodhisattva*s are said to dwell in celestial paradises, which the devotee can visit or desire to be reborn into.

Buddha A fully enlightened being; specifically, the historical Buddha Shakyamuni.

chaitya A temple or monastery hall.

chakravartin "Wheel-turner." An epithet of the Buddha; in Indian legend, either a world ruler or a great spiritual leader.

Chan (C.) "Meditation," from Sanskrit *dhyana*. The Chinese school of Buddhism from which Son (K.) and Zen (J.) derived.

chedi (Th.) The Thai form of the stupa.

chörten (T.) The Tibetan form of the stupa.

dagoba (Si.) The Sri Lankan form of the stupa.

deva A deity; either a major deity such as Brahma or Shiva, or a minor nature spirit.

Dharma (P. Dhamma) The Buddhist teaching; the "Middle Way" as taught by the Buddha.

duhkha (P. *dukkha*) Suffering: one of the Trilakshana (Three Characteristics of Existence), according to the Buddha. See also *anatman, anitya*.

dhyana (P. *jhyana*) "Meditation"; the origin of the Chinese word Chan, Japanese Zen, Korean Son, etc.

harmika The square platform on top of the classical Indian stupa, between the dome and the spire.

Jataka Any of more than five hundred popular legends of the Buddha's previous births.

Kannon, Kwannon (J.) See Avalokiteshvara.

karma (P. *kamma*) Action; the effects of action on the psyche, an impediment to enlightenment.

koan (J.) A riddle used in Rinzai Zen meditation; from C. *gong an*.

lama (T.) A spiritual teacher, translating the Sanskrit *guru*.

Linji (C.) A school of Chan Buddhism.

mandala A cosmogram, a representation of the Buddhist cosmos used as an aid in meditation. Often taking the form of a circle within a square and with a particular deity at the center, it is also understood as a "map" of the human psyche.

Mahayana "Great Vehicle," the tradition of Buddhism that is predominant in East Asia and Tibet. It is noted for the prominence given to the ideal of the *bodhisattva* and its distinctive doctrine of "emptiness." It is within the Mahayana that the schools of Chan (Zen) arose. See also *bodhisattva; shunyata*.

Maitreya A popular Mahayana *bodhisattva* revered as the next Buddha, a messianic savior who will appear in the future.

mantra Spoken or chanted sacred words or syllables repeated in Buddhist worship or meditation.

Mara The Evil One, the personification of desire or craving, who sought to tempt the Buddha in one final assault as he sat, on the verge of enlightenment.

Mon A people and culture which dominated the highlands and central plains of present-day Thailand and Burma from the sixth to eleventh centuries CE.

mudra A significant hand gesture used in meditation or teaching, an important element in Buddhist sculpture.

nirvana (P. *nibbana*) "Snuffing out," a timeless condition of spiritual freedom and awareness of reality that is the goal of Buddhist practice; to attain *nirvana* is to exit the cycle of *samsara*.

pagoda A name given to the forms of the stupa that developed in China and elsewhere, such as Thailand and Burma. The name may be a Portuguese version of Si. *dagoba*. See also *chedi*, *zedi*.

paramita "Perfection," any of six (later ten) virtues to be cultivated by the *bodhisattva*.

prajña (P. *panna*) "Wisdom," or "insight."

Rinzai (J.) A school of Zen Buddhism derived from Chinese Linji.

samsara Repeated rebirth (fueled by *karma*); unsatisfactory everyday reality; the opposite of *nirvana*.

Sangha The Buddhist monastic community, although it sometimes implies the entire community of Buddhist faithful.

Sanskrit An ancient Indian tongue that was the written language of classical Indian scripture and literature, and also of Mahayana Buddhism. Many Mahayana texts originally written in Sanskrit survive only

in translations into Chinese, Tibetan, or other languages.

satori (J.) Sudden enlightenment, in Japanese Zen practice.

Shakyamuni "Sage of the Shakya people," a title used in the Far East for the Buddha.

Shingon (J.) An esoteric form of Japanese Buddhism using *mantra*s, *mandala*s, and *mudra*s.

shunyata "Emptiness," the Absolute. The Mahayana doctrine of emptiness stresses that all phenomena, even the very concept of emptiness itself, are devoid of any intrinsic, permanent, identifying mark.

Siddhartha Gautama (P: Gotama) The Buddha's personal name.

Silk Road Extensive ancient trade routes linking northwest India, Central Asia, China, the Near East, and Europe.

Son (K.) The Korean school of meditation, from C. Chan. See also *dhyana*.

Soto (J.) A school of Zen Buddhism based on Chinese Caodong-zong.

stucco Plaster applied to exterior walls, often molded or decorated for visual effect.

stupa A domed reliquary mound built to enclose remains of Buddhist elders or sacred objects and texts. It developed many regional forms, such as the Sri Lankan *dagoba* and Chinese pagoda.

sutra Buddhist text, originally in Sanskrit or Pali, especially one attributed to the Buddha himself. See also *Tripitaka*.

Tantra See Vajrayana.

thangka (T.) In Tibetan Buddhism, a votive painting on a cloth scroll used in worship and meditation and depicting

deities, sacred beings, or holy persons such as celebrated *lama*s.

Theravada (P.) "Doctrine of the Elders," an ancient Indian school of Buddhism predominant in Sri Lanka and most of Southeast Asia.

Thien (V.) The Vietnamese school of meditation, from C. Chan. See also *dhyana*.

Trilakshana See *anatman*; *anitya*; *duhkha*.

Tripitaka (P. *Tipitaka*) The "Three Baskets," the oldest body of Buddhist teaching (*Sutra Pitaka*, *Vinaya Pitaka*, *Abhidharma Pitaka*), shared by all strands of Buddhism.

ushnisha "Wisdom bump" on the head of a representation of the Buddha or *bodhisattva*, indicating superior spiritual attainment.

Vairochana A powerful "cosmic Buddha," often represented in sculpture or in *mandala*s.

vajra (T. *dorje*) "Diamond Thunderbolt," an emblem of the supreme wisdom that is the goal of Buddhist practice.

Vajrayana "Diamond Vehicle," "Path of the Diamond Thunderbolt," an esoteric development of the Mahayana school in northern India that became prominent in Tibetan Buddhism. Also known as Tantra from the esoteric texts called *tantra*s.

vinaya Buddhist monastic discipline, as taught by the Buddha and laid down by the early Sangha. See also *Tripitaka*.

yaksha (m.) and *yakshi* (f.) A nature spirit of ancient Indian folklore, sometimes depicted in early Buddhist art and architecture.

zedi (B.) The Burmese form of the stupa.

Zen (J.) The Japanese school of "meditation only" Buddhism. See also Chan, *dhyana*.

BIBLIOGRAPHY

GENERAL

Bechert, H., and Gombrich, R. (eds.) *The World of Buddhism*. Thames and Hudson: London and New York, 1986.

Eliade, M. (ed.) *The Encyclopedia of Religion*. Macmillan: New York and London, 1987.

Fisher, Robert E. *Buddhist Art and Architecture*. Thames and Hudson: London and New York, 1993.

Gethin, Rupert. *The Foundations of Buddhism*. Oxford University Press: Oxford and New York, 1998.

Ghose, Rajeshwari. *In the Footsteps of the Buddha*. University Museum and Art Gallery, the University of Hong Kong: Hong Kong, 1998.

Harvey, P. *An Introduction to Buddhism*. Cambridge University Press: Cambridge, 1993.

Howard, Angelo Falco. *The Imagery of the Cosmological Buddha*. E.J. Brill: Leiden, 1986.

Seckel, Dietrich. *The Art of Buddhism*. Methuen: London, 1964.

De Silva-Vigier, Anil. *The Life of the Buddha: Retold from Ancient Sources*. Phaidon: London, 1955.

Trainor, Kevin. (ed.) *Buddhism: The Illustrated Guide*. Duncan Baird Publishers and Oxford University Press: London and New York, 2001.

Zwalf, W. *Buddhism: Art and Faith*. British Museum Publications: London, 1985.

CHAPTER 1 ORIGINS

Basham, A.L. *The Wonder that was India*. Grove Press: New York, 1959.

Carrithers, M. *The Buddha*. Oxford University Press: Oxford, 1983.

Conze, E. (ed.) *Buddhist Texts through the Ages*. Harper and Row: New York, 1964.

Conze E. (ed.) *Buddhist Scriptures*. Penguin: London and New York, 1973.

Ling, T. *The Buddha*. Penguin: London and New York, 1973.

Nyanaponika, Thera. *The Heart of Buddhist Meditation*. Weiser: New York, 1971.

Rahula, W. *What the Buddha Taught*. Wisdom Books: London, 1993.

Nyantiloka, Thera. *Buddhist Dictionary*. Buddhist Text Society: Kandy, Sri Lanka, 1986.

Warder, A.K. *Indian Buddhism*. Pali Text Society: Motilal Barnarsidas, New Delhi, 1980.

CHAPTER 2 INDIA AND CENTRAL ASIA

Along the Ancient Silk Routes: Central Asian Art from the West Berlin State Museums. The Metropolitan Museum of Art: New York, 1982.

Coomaraswamy, A.K.C. *History of Indian and Indonesian Art*. Dover: New York, 1988.

Kitagawa, J.M. (ed.) *Buddhism and Asian History*. Macmillan: New York, 1989.

Knox, R. *Amaravati: Buddhist Sculpture from the Great Stupa*. British Museum Press: London, 1992.

Michell, G. *Penguin Guide to the Monuments of India*. Penguin: London and New York, 1989.

Rowland, B. *The Art and Architecture of India*. Penguin: London, 1971 .

Whitfield, R., and Farrer, Anne. *Caves of the Thousand Buddhas: Chinese Art from the Silk Route*. British Museum Press: London, 1990.

Whitfield, S. *Life Along the Silk Road*. John Murray: London, 1999.

Zimmer, H. *The Art of Indian Asia*. Pantheon: New York 1955.

Zwalf, W. *Buddhism: Art and Faith*. British Museum Publications: London, 1985.

**CHAPTER 3 SRI LANKA AND
SOUTHEAST ASIA**

Gombrich, R. *Theravada Buddhism, A Social
History from Ancient Benares to Modern
Colombo*. Routledge: London, 1988.

Griswold, A.B. *Burma Korea Tibet*. Methuen:
London, 1964.

Johansson, R.E.A. *Pali Buddhist Texts
Explained to the Beginner*. Curzon Press:
London, 1977.

Keyes, Charles F. *The Golden Peninsula:
Culture and Adaptation in mainland Southeast
Asia*. University of Hawaii Press: Honolulu,
1995.

Swearer, Donald K. *The Buddhist World of
Southeast Asia*. State University of New York
Press: Albany, New York, 1995.

CHAPTER 4 EAST ASIA

Ch'en, K. *Buddhism in China*. Princeton
University Press: Princeton, New Jersey,
1973.

De Bary, T. (ed.) *Sources of Chinese Tradition*.
Columbia University Press: New York,
1960.

De Bary, T. (ed.) *Sources of Japanese
Tradition*. Columbia University Press: New
York, 1958.

Griswold, A.B. *Burma Korea Tibet*.
Methuen: London, 1964.

Mason, Penelope. *History of Japanese Art*.
Pearson Prentice Hall: New Jersey, 2005.

Stanley-Baker, J. *Japanese Art*. Thames and
Hudson: London, 1991.

Suzuki, D.T. *An Introduction to Zen
Buddhism*. Rider: London, 1983.

Wright, A.F. *Buddhism in Chinese History*.
Stanford University Press: Palo Alto,
California, 1959.

Yokoi, Y. Zen *Master Dogen*. Weatherhill:
New York and Tokyo, 1959.

**CHAPTER 5 THE HIMALAYAS
AND MONGOLIA**

Dagyab, Loden Sherap. *Tibetan Religious
Art*, 2 vols. Harrassowitz: Wiesbaden,
Germany, 1977.

Dalai Lama, H.H. the 14th. *The World of
Tibetan Buddhism*. Wisdom: Boston, 1995.

Gordon, A. *The Iconography of Tibetan
Lamaism*. Columbia University Press:
New York, 1939.

Griswold, A.B. *Burma Korea Tibet*.
Methuen: London, 1964.

Peacock, John. *The Tibetan Book of Life,
Death, and Rebirth*. Duncan Baird
Publishers: London, 2003.

Snellgrove, David, and Richardson,
Hugh. *A Cultural History of Tibet*.
Weidenfeld and Nicolson: London, 1968.

Willis, M. *Tibet: Life, Myth and Art*.
Duncan Baird Publishers: London, 1999.

INDEX

Note: Page references in *italics* refer to illustration captions, maps and plans.
Pali terms are given in brackets, for example: *anatman (anatta)*.

A

Abeyadana temple, Pagan 80
Abhayaghirivihara school 62
abhaya mudra see mudras
abhidharma 43,214, 215
Adam's Peak (Sripada) 68
Adibuddha (Primordial Buddha) 196, *198*
Adida Phat *see* Amitabha
Ahin Posh amulet *19*
Aizen *11*
Ajanta caves *39*, 50, 53
    Avalokiteshvara 50
    chaitya (shrine) hall 20
    monastic dwellings (*viharas*) 20
    recumbent Buddha 20
Akshobya Buddha 196–197, 210
Alchi, Ladakh 202
"all-seeing eyes" (Nepal) 210, 212
Amaravati stupa *13*, 22, *32*, *48*
Amida Buddha *see* Amitabha Buddha
Amidism (Japan) 165–168 *see also* Amitabha; Pure Land
Amitabha Buddha
    in China (Amituo Fo) 116, 118, 120, *122*, *133*
    in Japan (Amida Butsu) *155*, *156*, *166*, *167*, *168*
    in Tibet *183*, 196, *196*
    in Vietnam (Adida Phat) 176, *176*, *179*
Amitabha Sutra 142
Amoghasiddhi Buddha *196–197*
amulet *19*
Ananda (disciple of Buddha) 35, Thailand *61*
Ananda (Burmese temple) *2*, *78*, 80
anatman (anatta) 28
Anawrahta (Anuruddha), King 73–75, 78, *80*, 83
anda (stupa dome) *see* stupa
Angkor Thom 90, 96–99
    apsaras 98
    Avalokiteshvara 98
    Bayon temple 93, 96–98, *97*, *98*
    Neak Pean *92*
    Suryavarman I, King 96
    Terrace of the Elephants *93*, 96
    Terrace of the Leprous King 98
    Yasovarman I, King 96
Angkor Wat 93, 96
anitya (anicca) 28
Anuradhapura 62, 66
    Buddha *62*
    Ruwanweliseya *dagoba 10*, 69
    Sri Maha Bodhi 69
Anuruddha, King *see* Anawrahta, King
apsaras 98
arahat, arhat 36, 214,
Ashoka, Emperor 44–45
    Sañchi stupa 48
    Nepal 208
    Sri Lanka, mission to 62
Asia, map *7*
Aukana 68
Avalokiteshvara
    in Cambodia (Lokeshvara) *91*, 92, *92*
        Angkor Thom *92*, 98
    in China (Guanyin) 8, *26*, *106*, 110, 114, *117*, 120
        cult of 120
        Dunhuang *26*, *114*, *117*
        feminization of, as Guanyin 8, *122*, 128
    as emanation of Amitabha 120, 197

Avalokiteshvara (cont.)
    in India *50*, *71*
    in Japan (Kannon/Kwannon) 147, *159*
    in Korea (Kwanum) *138*
    in Nepal 210
    in Sri Lanka (Lokeshvara) 62, *63*
    in Thailand (Lokeshvara) 85
    in Tibet (Chenrezi) 8, 182, *183*, *184*, 194, 196, 197
        mantra of 182
    in Vietnam (Lokeshvara) *176*, *179*
Ayutthaya *82*, 83, 85, *85*, 86, *86 see also* Thailand
    Ayutthaya period carvings *86*

B

Bamiyan *57*, 58
Bardo Thodol (*Tibetan Book of the Dead*) 186
bark manuscripts 43–44
Bayon temple, Angkor Thom 93, 96–98, *97*, *98*
Bezeklik 58
Bharhut stupa 22, 24, *24–25*
bhikshus 32 *see also* Sangha, *vinaya*
bhumisparsamudra see mudras
Bhutan 202, 203, *204*, 204–205,
Big Wild Goose pagoda 111
Bodhgaya 52, 214
bodhi 22
Bodhi Tree 22, *24*, *48–49*, 52, 214
Bodhidharma 121, *160*, 163
bodhisattvas
    in Mahayana Buddhism 9–10
    representation of 8
        Bhutanese 204
        Chinese 8, *107*, *110*, *114*, *115*, *116*, *119*, *122*,
        Gandharan *40*
        Indian 24, *48-49*
        Japanese 147, *155*, *157*, *158*, *159*, *165*, *166*
        Khmer *91*, *97*
        Korean *138*, *140*, *142*
        Nepalese 210
        Thai 85
        Tibetan 8, *183*, *194*,
        Vietnamese 76, *79*
    in Theravada Buddhism 10, 62, *63*, 85
    see also Avalokiteshvara *and other individual names*
Bodhisattva, the *see* Buddha
Bo Juyi 127
book illustration *71*, *88*, 186, *187*, 212
Borobudur 100–105, *102*, *103*, *104*, *105*
Brahma 92
British colonialism 66, 77, 202
bronze water vessels (Korea) *139*
Buddha, the
    birth 14, *14*, 202, *209*
    as the Bodhisattva *16*, 72, *80*, 127
    enlightenment (awakening) 16, 17, 95 *see also* meditat-
        ing *under* representation *subentry*
    death *see parinirvana*
    Jatakas 24, *153*,
    life 14–25
    relics *32*, 35, 126
    representation 6, 8, 22–25
        Bhutanese 204
        Burmese *2*, *72*, 75–76, *75*, *76*, *80*, *100*
        Central Asian *58*
        Chinese *26*, *109*, *119*, 120, 121–122, *132*,
        132, 134

Buddha, the (cont.)
    representations (cont.)
        eternal 121–122
        fasting *16*
        Gandharan *16*, *19*
        Indian *20*, 24–25, *26*, *53*
        Japanese *153*, *158*, *165*
        Javanese *101*, *102*, *105*
        Khmer 92
        Korean 145, *145*
        Laotian 95, *95*
        meditating *17*, *53*, 62, 74, *85*, *86*, *95*, *102*, 132,
        132, 145, 145
        Nepalese *210*, *212*
        parinirvana 20, 66, *149*
        preaching *109*, *112*, 142
        Sri Lankan 35, *62*, 66, *68*, 69
        standing *2*, *76*, 109
        in symbolic form 6, 8, *12*, 22–25, *192*
        Thai *61*, *83*, *85*, *86*, 95
        Tibetan , *192*
        walking *83*
    teachings of 26–31
    see also mudras; relics; Siddhartha
Buddha's tooth relic 68, 75, 78
Buddhaghosa 63
Buddhaisawan temple *88*
Buddhanath stupa (Nepal) *210–211*
Buddhapada see footprints (*Buddhapada*)
Buddhas *see* Buddha, the *and other individual names*
Burma 72–77
    Ananda temple *78*, 80
    British colonization 77
    Buddha representations *72*, *74*, 75–76, *76*
    Buddha's tooth replica 75, 78
    cotton tapestry *72*
    disunity and revival 76–77
    Dvaravati kingdom 73
    glazed pottery tiles 73, *73*
    Konbaung dynasty 77
    Kuthodaw pagoda 77
    Mahayana Buddhism 73
        chakravartin Buddha 76
    Mindon, King 77
    Mon kingdom 72, 76–77
    Pagan (Bagan) *see separate entry*
    script 70
    Shwezigon *see separate entry*
    Sri Lanka, links with 75
    stupa (*zedi*) 76
    Tantric Buddhism 73
    Theravada Buddhism 73, 75
    Tibeto-Burmese people 73
    Toungoo dynasty 77
    written records 71
Byzantium *130*

C

calligraphy *130 see also* manuscripts
Cambodia 90–94
    Angkor 83, 90, 91, 92, 93, *93*, 96–98, *96*, *97*, *98*,
    102
    Angkor Thom *see separate entry*
    Angkor Wat 93, 96
    architecture 92–93
    Avalokiteshvara *bodhisattva 91*

ACKNOWLEDGMENTS AND PICTURE CREDITS

Acknowledgments

This book could not have been written without Peter Bently who has contributed prodigious quantities of time in addition to skill and specialist knowledge to the content and direction of each chapter. Many thanks also to Christopher Westhorp, for his constantly helpful advice and editorial management, and to Julia Ruxton, for her wide-ranging and always illuminating picture research. *Tom Lowenstein.*

The publisher would like to thank Tom Lowenstein and Peter Bently for their coordinated, skilled and authoritative authorship of the separate chapters of this work; in addition, gratitude is expressed to John Peacocke for casting a diligent expert's eye over the work as a whole, and to Todd Lewis for his valuable expertise on Nepal.